Occupied

The Channel Islands were the only territory in the British Isles captured by the forces of Nazi Germany in the Second World War. Despite many books, television programmes and film dramas on the subject, people are still surprised to learn what happened in the islands between 1940 and 1945. Islanders faced a very different war to the rest of Britain, or those parts of Europe that became battlefields. Liberation came at the stroke of a pen rather than armed assault.

Whilst a slim majority of islanders remained to face the uncertainty of occupation, almost half chose to be evacuated to England or join the British armed forces. Of those who remained in Guernsey and Sark, a thousand were deported to internment camps in Germany. Anyone who defied the Nazis risked arrest, imprisonment, or torture or death in a continental Nazi prison, labour or concentration camp. These different groups of islanders had contrasting experiences, and between Guernsey, Sark and Alderney there is no single story of the Occupation.

This book is an introduction to the Occupation, using the archives of Guernsey Museum. It concentrates on the Bailiwick of Guernsey, which includes the islands of Alderney, Sark and Herm; space does not permit much discussion of events in

(right)
German military band march past Lloyd's Bank in St Peter Port

(below)
German soldier inside a Guernsey greenhouse.

Carel Toms

the Bailiwick of Jersey. Both Bailiwicks are self-governing 'Crown Dependencies', loyal to the English Crown, but although British are not part of the United Kingdom. Each has a Bailiff as the chief civil official, an elected 'States' or parliament to run the government and, in 1940, a Lieutenant-Governor representing the King. Alderney also has its own States, and Sark has a semi-feudal system of government. The curious constitutional arrangement dates back to the reign of King John in 1204 and ultimately to the Norman Conquest of England in 1066. The fact that the islands are not ruled from London starts to explain the chaos, confusion and tragedy that unfolded during the war.

A Quiet War

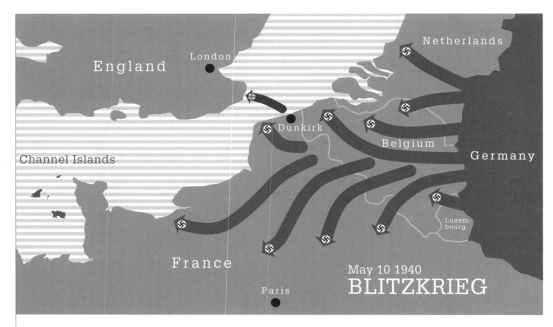

May 10 1940
BLITZKRIEG

Britain declared war on Nazi Germany in September 1939 following the invasion of Poland by the German army. Some Channel Islanders were already serving in the British forces and others volunteered in the early months of the war. Guernsey and Jersey also made generous contributions of money to help the war effort. By ancient custom, men of the islands could not be conscripted into the forces against their will, but Britain and the Islands' States started to discuss creating laws to make it possible. Nobody seemed to be in a hurry and the dramatic events of June 1940 stopped the laws ever becoming effective. Meanwhile the few German, Italian and Austrian residents were interned as 'enemy aliens' in late May 1940.

At first the German army concentrated on defeating the Poles, and Britain and its allies did little to stop them. Although Britain declared war in September 1939, its army did not engage that of the Germans, and so late 1939 and early 1940 became known as the 'Phoney War'. Britain did not regard the Channel Islands as being strategically important and thought there was little danger they would be attacked. Most of the garrison troops were withdrawn as the men were needed elsewhere, and the Royal Guernsey Militia was weakened as men volunteered to join the regulars. Island governments asked for artillery to defend the coasts and anti-aircraft guns, searchlights and machine guns to defend the airports but London was unable to help. Weapons were in short supply and the Islands would have to pay for any guns they received.

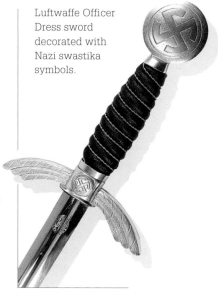

Luftwaffe Officer Dress sword decorated with Nazi swastika symbols.

In April 1940 the Phoney War ended when Allied troops were driven out of Norway by a German invasion. British Prime Minister Neville Chamberlain resigned and was replaced by Winston Churchill. On May 10th, the Germans launched their *'Blitzkrieg'* against the Netherlands, Luxembourg and Belgium. These countries quickly fell, and the Germans also launched an unexpected attack through the Ardennes into France. French armies trying to stop the offensive suffered a stunning defeat, and the small British Expeditionary Force was driven back until trapped against the Channel coast. Most but not all survivors were evacuated from the port of Dunkirk just in time to escape complete destruction; many others were taken as prisoners of war. German forces swept through France and Paris was declared an Open City to stop it becoming a battleground. It fell to the Nazis on June 14th.

When France made an armistice with the Germans on June 22nd, the Channel Islands suddenly became vulnerable. Discussions between the States' and different departments of the British government see-sawed as to whether the islands should be defended or evacuated. Arguments raged over whether there would be enough food, fuel and medicine to supply people who stayed, or who would pay for ships to take islanders to safety.

Small bronze bust of German Führer Adolf Hitler. Portraits of Hitler commonly decorated buildings and offices taken over by the Germans.

British and French soldiers passed through the islands after being evacuated from St Malo. As smoke could be seen from the French coasts and refugees started to reach St Peter Port in any boat they could find, an air of panic started to set in amongst islanders. German *Luftwaffe* aircraft soon occupied French airbases within easy striking range, and it was clear that the islands would be devastated by bombers if there was any attempt to defend them. This indeed was what the German navy planned as the opening stage of what they called Operation *Grüne Pfeile* (Green Arrows). Next would come simultaneous invasions of Alderney and Guernsey, followed by Jersey, using up to six battalions of soldiers. Resistance would be quickly crushed.

After losing so many troops, ships and aircraft in France, the British finally decided that the islands could not be defended, and that if the Germans occupied them it would simply waste their resources. The British withdrew their last troops by June 20th, and on the 22nd the King wrote to the Bailiffs of both Guernsey and Jersey wishing them well and regretting the need to leave them undefended. The Royal Guernsey Militia was disbanded, and the islands awaited invasion.

No Cause For Panic

The rapidly changing news caused confusion in the islands. Some people wanted to escape to England straight away, others were determined to stay whatever happened, but many families were undecided. Local doctors advised that the islands should be completely evacuated, as medicines would soon run short. Nobody had drawn up a plan for an evacuation, official opinion changed from one day to the next and advice was contradictory. To try to quell the growing panic Guernsey officials started to recommend that people stay and see things through, especially essential workers, medical staff and police.

A sudden announcement was made on June 19th that ships would arrive to evacuate civilians from Guernsey, starting with school children and men of military age. People who wished to leave needed to register, but in the end many who wished to go were left behind and others changed their minds and went at the last minute. Over the following week 17,000 people left Guernsey for England, leaving 25,000 behind. Families were split, with some members leaving first and others then unable to follow. Pets were destroyed or set loose and some farmers shot their animals before leaving. People buried their valuables and pubs gave away free drinks which just added to the chaos. After the war it was a common view that if everyone had known the occupation would last so long, few would have chosen to stay.

Unofficial poster opposing evacuation, June 1940.

(above left)
Head of spent bullet which narrowly missed a family having tea in the Grange on June 28th 1940.

Communications between Guernsey and Alderney broke down, leaving residents of the smaller island unsure what was happening. They could see enemy troops on the French coast only nine miles away and exhausted French soldiers arrived in small boats after escaping from Cherbourg. When the British garrison suddenly began leaving on June 16th it increased the alarm, and some civilians found the opportunity to go in the next few days. Alderney States' President Judge French called a meeting, and the islanders voted to leave. On June 23rd, almost the entire population of 1,436 left for England on six ships with only the possessions they could carry. Only a handful decided stubbornly to remain.

Sark is a place apart. The island was led by the formidable Dame of Sark, the feudal seigneur Sibyl Hathaway who encouraged everyone who could to stay. Some English residents decided to return home, but 471 stayed put including all the native Sarkees and the Dame's American husband.

The Lieutenant-Governor was recalled to Britain, leaving the Bailiff Victor Carey as his deputy. Democracy was unlikely to be allowed under the Nazis, but the islands still needed a government even if they were occupied, so Guernsey formed a

NOTICE.

I am instructed to inform the people of Guernsey that the Government of the United Kingdom has decided that this Bailiwick is to be entirely demilitarised.

Accordingly, the Royal Court hereby gives instructions for the immediate demobilisation of the Royal Guernsey Militia and of the Guernsey Defence Volunteers.

Arms, uniforms and equipment are forthwith to be handed in at the Town Arsenal under arrangements to be made by the Officers Commanding the Royal Guernsey Militia and the Guernsey Defence Volunteers, to be disposed of in accordance with the instructions of the Officer Commanding Troops Guernsey and Alderney District.

All ranks of the Militia and all members of the Guernsey Defence Volunteers will then proceed quietly to their homes.

All other persons in possession of firearms must forthwith hand them to the Constable of their Parish who will take immediate steps to have them transported to the Town Arsenal.

VICTOR G. CAREY,
Bailiff of Guernsey.

Official Notice of demilitarisation issued by the Royal Court.

'Controlling Committee' led by Procureur (Attorney General) Ambrose Sherwill. This would allow much faster decision-making in a time of crisis and give the Germans less excuse to impose a government of 'Quisling' collaborators. Island life would continue as normal as possible for as long as possible. Horticulture was a major part of the economy and one urgent job was to make sure the tomato crop was shipped to England whilst there was still time.

Although the islands had been demilitarised, the Germans claimed not to have been told. The British had been too embarrassed to make the news public and even the King's letter was not to be published. All this muddle led to tragedy. German planes flew reconnaissance flights over the islands and could not see evidence they were still defended, but German officers planning Operation Green Arrows were wary of falling into a trap, so they ordered a 'reconnaissance in force' against the islands. *Luftwaffe* bombers would attack St Peter Port and St Helier to see whether defending troops fired back. On June 28th six Heinkel He 111 bombers approached Guernsey and three swooped on St Peter Port harbour at low level, machine guns blazing and dropping bombs. People scattered to find cover, some hiding under tomato lorries queuing to be unloaded. Whether or not the pilots mistook these for military trucks, they bombed them anyway and left the wrecks burning. 34 civilians were killed, and 11 more when the bombers turned their attention to Jersey. PC 'Chipper' Bougourd and ambulance driver

(above left)
Smoke rises from burning trucks by St Peter Port harbour, 28th June 1940.

(above)
Harold Hobbs.

(top)
Naval cap band worn by Harold Hobbs.

Joseph Way died when a clearly marked ambulance was attacked. Harold Hobbs, son of the coxswain, was killed at sea when the Guernsey Lifeboat was machine-gunned. Spreading terror was a deliberate tactic of the *Blitzkrieg*.

The only response came from a single machine-gun on the ferry *Isle of Sark*, but German planners were still suspicious that the British might have artillery well-hidden, so ordered a second mission. It never took place as, on June 30th, a daring pilot from the *Luftwaffe* noticed that Guernsey airport was deserted and landed to discover the island was truly undefended. The *Luftwaffe* immediately flew in a small number of troops on Junkers transport planes and Guernsey's Inspector of Police handed over a letter surrendering the island to the invaders. Irritated that the *Luftwaffe* had shortcut their plans, the German navy flew in more troops on July 1st. As the runway in Alderney had been blocked, and there was no government left to offer submission, it was July 2nd before a landing was made and July 4th before German troops landed there by sea. For the rest of the war, the Channel Islands were occupied by the enemy.

The weighbridge at St Peter Port harbour left in ruins following the air raid.

The so-called
"Model Occupation"

The Occupation began quietly, and German troops behaved well considering the stories of atrocities that emerged following the invasions of Poland, Holland and Belgium. German Führer Adolf Hitler wanted to use the occupation of the Channel Islands for propaganda, and to show the British people how civilised the Germans could be. In June 1940 he still hoped that Britain would make peace, and if not it would be crushed by the *Luftwaffe* and then invaded.

Once the shock of seeing troops in field grey uniforms marching down island streets had subsided, life settled down to an uneasy understanding between islanders and occupiers. Ambrose Sherwill expressed the vain hope it would be a "Model Occupation" but later regretted the positive tone of his message.

Islanders were now reliant on German goodwill to ensure they had food, fuel, water and medicines. Polite as the occupiers seemed, everyone knew they would deal harshly with anyone who opposed them, although at that stage of the war people did not know the extent of barbarity the Nazis were capable of.

For their part, the Germans also needed to keep the islanders docile. It would make security easier and help maintain that neat propaganda image. They needed islanders to continue running essential services, grow food, supply milk, keep the power station running and police themselves. It was important that everyone remained in good health to achieve this, and any epidemic that struck the civilians would strike the military too.

(above)
German soldiers in Sark pose for the photographer.

(right)
An illicit camera records captured French tanks in St Martins.

Frank Le Page

German troops marching up the Lower Pollet.

In August 1940, the German military government, *Feldkommandantur* 515, took over administration of the islands, which were treated as part of France. It was based in Jersey and had a branch or *Nebenstelle* in Guernsey with a mix of military and civilian staff. Civilian government was allowed to continue, but all decisions needed to be approved by the *Feldkommandantur*. The Germans would also pass down orders which they wanted the islands to put into law. Whilst Guernsey officials could argue points of detail, beyond a point they had little option but comply or resign and the Controlling Committee's work was repeatedly impeded by interference by German officials. The States had to double

income tax to pay for the costs of being occupied, and arguments would flow between officials of both sides over the costs of the Occupation such as the billeting of troops which even Sark was expected to bear.

We imagine the Germans as being efficient, but the Nazis had a deliberately complicated command structure and the various civilian, military and political organisations often disagreed with each other. Rivalry between senior officers was rife and their administration was often incompetent. Military command was based in Guernsey and for much of the war fell under the *Befehlshaber* Count von Schmettow, an old-school Prussian officer who lost a lung

"

It was never a matter of being soft but of being sensible. I felt when I was given the command that if the people acted correctly, I could instil into my troops strict and correct behaviour."

Befehlshaber Count von Schmettow

(above)
The German flag hangs over Guernsey airport.

(above right)
German *Luftwaffe* troops march along Glategny Esplanade, St Peter Port.

German Field Post Office sign.

German troops photographed in St Martins by an illicit camera.

in the First World War. Islanders benefitted from his humane and practical approach to the Occupation, but hardcore Nazis criticised him for being too soft. After the war he said "It was never a matter of being soft but of being sensible. I felt when I was given the command that if the people acted correctly, I could instil into my troops strict and correct behaviour."

Frank Le Page

German sign prohibiting access to Fermain.

Verboten!

Occupied Guernsey immediately changed to the Central European time zone. An early order from the Germans was for all weapons to be handed in, which the island authorities were keen to enforce as a single incident was feared to be enough to trigger heavy reprisals. At first people were allowed to keep their radio sets and the BBC was a source of contact with the outside world, although the war news was grim in 1940-41. Radios were temporarily confiscated following the discovery of British agents in the island in late 1940, then taken away completely in June 1942 due to German fears over the BBC encouraging resistance in Europe.

Cunning islanders responded initially by ignoring the order and later by making crystal radio sets, which needed no power and could be easily concealed. Minerals were even taken from the Museum's geology collection to provide the crystals and earpieces were stolen from phone boxes. Ingenious methods were devised to hide the crystal sets: under floorboards,

in secret cupboards and in an emergency even such places as a saucepan on the stove or in a child's pram. Even the Dame of Sark had her own hidden set. The Germans launched searches for clandestine radios, and shamefully some residents informed on their neighbours in order to settle petty squabbles. More traditional German officers disliked relying on traitors, and some are said to have ignored anonymous notes or passed the word to the local police who quietly destroyed the most vindictive tip-offs.

The Germans requisitioned private cars for their own use, and to keep islanders from moving around. Restrictions increased as supplies of petrol grew short and only essential use was allowed for those such as doctors and lorry drivers. Islanders turned to the bicycle, but the Germans also demanded a quota of bicycles for use by their troops. In June 1941 the rules of the road were changed so that everyone had to drive on the right, as on the continent. German traffic signs started to appear, and places were

(above)
German sign prohibiting spitting inside a vehicle.

(right)
Bottom of St Julian's Avenue, St Peter Port, with German censor, Sonderführer Kurt Goettmann, 1943.

given German names. Castle Cornet became *Hafenschloss* and the route from St Julian's Avenue to the Rohais became *Hochstrasse*.

Both *The Guernsey Evening Press* and *The Star* continued to be published, but were heavily censored. The front pages were essentially German propaganda, so news was replaced in part by rumour spread in the ration-queue. The Germans issued flurries of orders. It became an offence to utter words that would offend German troops, or to assemble in groups, and Germans had to be served before civilians in shops. Cameras were confiscated in July 1942. 'Forbidden' books by authors despised by the Nazis were supposed to be handed in, but were chiefly just hidden; especially at the Priaulx library.

It was still common for Guernseymen to own a small boat for fishing or taking crabs, even if not full-time fishermen. This way of life became difficult due to German fears of islanders escaping, which a few indeed succeeded in doing. All boats were gathered from the coasts to the main harbours of St Peter Port or St Sampsons. German policy swung back and forth, banning fishing, then restricting times boats could set out, then insisting that a guard accompany the boats, then only permitting licensed fishermen to go out after paying deposits for good behaviour and taking a percentage of each catch. With shore gathering and rod-fishing also highly restricted, all this reduced the effectiveness of fishing and made both fish and crabs scarce in the markets.

(above)
German Road Signs Instruction Notice. These regulations came into force on 25th July 1942.

(right)
Orders of the German Commandant published on 1st July 1940 and reproduced in the *Guernsey Evening Press*.

REGISTERED AT THE G.P.O. AS A NEWSPAPER   POSTAGE ½d   GUERNSEY, MONDAY, JULY 1, 1940   TELEPHONE 1400 (FIVE LINES)

ORDERS OF THE COMMANDANT OF THE GERMAN FORCES IN OCCUPATION OF THE ISLAND OF GUERNSEY

(1)—ALL INHABITANTS MUST BE INDOORS BY 11 P.M. AND MUST NOT LEAVE THEIR HOMES BEFORE 6 A.M.

(2)—WE WILL RESPECT THE POPULATION IN GUERNSEY; BUT, SHOULD ANYONE ATTEMPT TO CAUSE THE LEAST TROUBLE, SERIOUS MEASURES WILL BE TAKEN AND THE TOWN WILL BE BOMBED.

(3)—ALL ORDERS GIVEN BY THE MILITARY AUTHORITY ARE TO BE STRICTLY OBEYED.

(4)—ALL SPIRITS MUST BE LOCKED UP IMMEDIATELY, AND NO SPIRITS MAY BE SUPPLIED, OBTAINED OR CONSUMED HENCEFORTH. THIS PROHIBITION DOES NOT APPLY TO STOCKS IN PRIVATE HOUSES.

(5)—NO PERSON SHALL ENTER THE AERODROME AT LA VILLIAZE.

(6)—ALL RIFLES, AIRGUNS, PISTOLS, REVOLVERS, DAGGERS, SPORTING GUNS, AND ALL OTHER WEAPONS WHATSOEVER, EXCEPT SOUVENIRS, MUST, TOGETHER WITH ALL AMMUNITION, BE DELIVERED AT THE ROYAL HOTEL BY 12 NOON TO-DAY, JULY 1.

(7)—ALL BRITISH SAILORS, AIRMEN AND SOLDIERS ON LEAVE IN THIS ISLAND MUST REPORT AT THE POLICE STATION AT 9 A.M. TO-DAY, AND MUST THEN REPORT AT THE ROYAL HOTEL.

(8)—NO BOAT OR VESSEL OF ANY DESCRIPTION, INCLUDING ANY FISHING BOAT, SHALL LEAVE THE HARBOURS OR ANY OTHER PLACE WHERE THE SAME IS MOORED, WITHOUT AN ORDER FROM THE MILITARY AUTHORITY, TO BE OBTAINED AT THE ROYAL HOTEL. ALL BOATS ARRIVING FROM JERSEY, FROM SARK OR FROM HERM, OR ELSEWHERE, MUST REMAIN IN HARBOUR UNTIL PERMITTED BY THE MILITARY TO LEAVE.

THE CREWS WILL REMAIN ON BOARD. THE MASTER WILL REPORT TO THE HARBOURMASTER, ST. PETER-PORT, AND WILL OBEY HIS INSTRUCTIONS.

(9)—THE SALE OF MOTOR SPIRIT IS PROHIBITED, EXCEPT FOR USE ON ESSENTIAL SERVICES, SUCH AS DOCTORS' VEHICLES, THE DELIVERY OF FOODSTUFFS, AND SANITARY SERVICES WHERE SUCH VEHICLES ARE IN POSSESSION OF A PERMIT FROM THE MILITARY AUTHORITY TO OBTAIN SUPPLIES.

THESE VEHICLES MUST BE BROUGHT TO THE ROYAL HOTEL BY 12 NOON TO-DAY TO RECEIVE THE NECESSARY PERMISSION.

THE USE OF CARS FOR PRIVATE PURPOSES IS FORBIDDEN.

(10)—THE BLACK-OUT REGULATIONS ALREADY IN FORCE MUST BE OBSERVED AS BEFORE.

(11)—BANKS AND SHOPS WILL BE OPEN AS USUAL.

(Signed) THE GERMAN COMMANDANT OF THE ISLAND OF GUERNSEY

JULY 1, 1940.

Commandos and Spies

British Prime Minister Sir Winston Churchill wanted to strike back against the Occupiers in response to the humiliation of having given up the islands so hastily. A series of military operations were launched, but most were planned too quickly or too optimistically and hovered between farce and tragedy.

On July 6th 1940, Guernseyman Lieutenant Hubert Nicolle was brought by submarine on a spying mission. He landed at Jaonnet Bay on the south coast, despite his canoe overturning. Nicolle was relieved by Lieutenants Martel and Mulholland three nights later, surviving again when his return boat was swamped. Operation 'Ambassador' was to follow on July 14th, with the officers already ashore guiding 140 Commandos to raid the airport and knock out German look-out positions on Jerbourg. Bad weather delayed the attack,

then problems with the launches carrying the men and difficulties navigating in the dark meant that only one group made it ashore. Landing at Petit Port, the commandos found no German look-out point to capture. Instead they built a hasty roadblock using stones from a garden, attempted to cut telephone wires and retreated to the beach. Again, a boat overturned, three non-swimmers were left behind and another man fell into the sea and was taken prisoner.

Martel and Mulholland meanwhile hid until it was clear they were not going to escape. They went to Sherwill who had them dressed in Royal Guernsey Militia uniforms before they surrendered, in the hope this would stop them being shot as spies. They were sent to France and then various PoW camps in Europe. Two women accused of assisting them were sent to France for six months.

(above)
Portrait of
Lt Desmond
Mulholland by
Arthur C. Michael.

(top left)
Submarine H43
that delivered
Lt Hubert Nicolle
on his first mission.

Priaulx Library

(right)
Lt Hubert Nicolle
shown as a PoW.

Churchill was not impressed by the "silly fiasco", but it did not deter further operations. Sergeant Stanley Ferbrache landed in August and tried in vain to find the missing men before he himself was successfully rescued. In September Nicolle returned, landing at Petit Port in company with Second Lieutenant Symes. Their mission was to discover as much as they could about the German garrison and the situation of islanders. It proved impossible to bring the men back, so they hid for five weeks with friends and relations. Captain Parker was the next to land to prepare for Operation 'Tomato', a 750-man raid on the islands, but he was immediately captured and 'Tomato' never happened.

In October the Germans announced that all British soldiers still in Guernsey must hand themselves in by the 21st. After that date they would be treated as spies and probably shot. Relatives found uniforms for Nicolle and Symes and they surrendered at St Peter Port Police Station on the day the ultimatum expired. Although the two men were clearly spies, Von Schmettow intervened and ensured they were treated as Prisoners of War. To punish islanders for helping the men, radios were confiscated and fifteen of their friends and relations as well as Ambrose Sherwill were arrested and sent to France. Symes' father died in the Cherche Midi prison in Paris in unconfirmed circumstances. The others returned to the island in January, Sherwill was banned from holding public office and the deported men were relieved of their jobs.

Poster warning British troops still remaining in the islands to hand themselves in.

NOTICE

Members of the British Armed Forces in hiding in Guernsey and persons who are assisting them in any way must report at the Island Police Station, St. Peter-Port at the latest by

6 P.M. ON MONDAY, 21st. OCTOBER 1940.

Members of the British Armed Forces obeying this order will be treated as prisoners of war and no measures will be taken against persons who have assisted them.

Any Member of the British Armed Forces who may be found after this time limit must expect to be treated as an agent of an enemy power. Also all those who have assisted in hiding such persons or in any other way will have to take the full consequences of such actions.

Feldkommandantur 515
Nebenstelle Guernsey.

i.V. Signed. DR. BROSCH.

Guernsey, 18th October, 1940.

BEKANNTMACHUNG

Britische Wehrmachtsangehörige, die sich auf Guernsey verborgen halten und Personen, die ihnen in irgendeiner Weise Beistand leisten, haben sich

BIS SPÄTESTENS 21. OKTOBER 1940, 18 UHR

bei der Insel-Polizei in St. Peter-Port zu melden.

Britische Wehrmachtsangehörige, die sich bis zu diesem Zeitpunkt melden, werden als Kriegsgefangene behandelt; gegen diejenigen Personen, die ihnen Beistand geleistet haben, werden keinerlei Massnahmen ergriffen werden.

Britische Wehrmachtsangehörige, die nach diesem Zeitpunkt festgestellt werden, müssen gewärtig sein, als Agenten einer feindlichen Macht behandelt zu werden; auch werden diejenigen zu strenger Rechenschaft gezogen werden, die ihnen bei der Verbergung oder in irgendeiner anderen Weise Beistand geleistet haben.

Feldkommandantur 515
Nebenstelle Guernsey.

i.V.gez. DR. BROSCH.

Guernsey, den 18.Oktober 1940.

Star Typ., Bordage.

Occupied Life

Food was the major worry for islanders. There was never enough, and it was poor quality. The Controlling Committee published an Occupation Cookbook containing simplified recipes possible on the declining rations and aimed to reduce the amount of fuel needed for cooking. A Purchasing Commission was also established in France at the port of Granville. The Guernsey representative was Raymond Falla who developed essential talents for arguing with the Germans and "swearing in French". He would buy whatever could be obtained, including flour, tinned pork and even willow to make crabpots, and in return Guernsey would send tomatoes.

People stockpiled food at the start of the Occupation, but gradually these stocks ran down and there were serious shortages by the end of 1941. Country folk fared better than poorer townsfolk and anyone with land

attempted to grow food where they could. White bread was replaced by the heavy 'Occupation Loaf' made from 50% potato flour. Eggs were in short supply due to the lack of poultry feed and there was often no cheese at all. Only skimmed milk was available for adults and the meat ration declined to one ounce a week per person by 1944, which in practice could mean none at all. The Guernsey diet became more and more reliant on vegetables, but ironically some aspects of health improved initially due to the shortage of fat, sugar, tobacco and alcohol.

As stocks ran out, ingenious substitutes were adopted which ranged from the adequate to

(top)
Queuing for Collins Shop sweets, St Peter Port.

(above)
Example of a fuel ration card.

No. 588 A1

The holder of this Card is / Inhaber dieser Karte ist) BRIAND MARIE

Residing at / Wohnhaft) 2b HAVILLAND St ST PETER PORT

Born on the / Geboren am) at / in) FRANCE

PARTICULARS — NÄHERE ANGAB

...Single, Married, Widow or Widower / ...Ledig, verheiratet, verwitwet

...Colour of Hair / ...Farbe des Haares

...Colour of Eyes / ...Farbe der Augen

Controlling Committee of the States of Guernsey,

Feldkommandantur, Nebenstelle Guernsey.

Some vehicles were adopted to run on 'Gasogene' made from coal. Oil was needed to heat the greenhouses and coal to keep the power station running and to manufacture gas, which was widely used for cooking and lighting. As the gas supply dwindled, it was turned off in the evening. Families would sit in the dark unless they used precious candles, and the ration was a single candle per week. Firewood was rationed and the Germans stopped trees being felled that camouflaged their positions. Teachers complained that their pupils could no longer concentrate as the schools were so cold.

disgusting. Bramble leaf tea, jelly made from seaweed, coffee from ground parsnips and 'tobacco' made by drying tealeaves were all attempted. An inferior tobacco was grown locally, grapes were grown in vineries to produce a Guernsey wine and the brewery carried on making beer of decreasing strength using whatever ingredients were available. Parsnips and limpets were previously despised foods that now found a market. 'Sugar beet' provided a substitute sugar and purified seawater was used for cooking when salt ran short.

Fuel was also in short supply and petrol became scarce for even essential drivers.

IDENTITY CARD
—
IDENTITAETSKARTE

Star Typ.

All adult islanders had to carry identity cards

(right)
Ration queue in Fountain Street

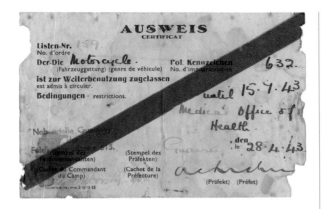

In the early weeks of the Occupation, German soldiers went on a shopping spree, stripping the shops of goods that would be needed later in the war. British currency continued to be used alongside Reichsmarks. Germans sent local coins home as souvenirs so that there was eventually a shortage and notes had to be printed with a value as low as one penny. When the supply of one penny stamps ran out, two penny stamps were cut diagonally in half.

With no re-supply, shops soon ran out of things to sell. Once the shelves were empty, islanders took to bartering and adverts appeared in the newspapers offering, for example, a saucepan in exchange for a bicycle tyre. Children's clothes could be swapped as they grew out of them and needed bigger sizes. 'Make do and mend' was essential as adult clothes were cut down for children and worn-out garments unpicked to recover the wool and thread. Leather bags were cut up to make shoes. Some shops acted as centres for bartering or held auctions, with the shopkeeper making a little profit. Gradually the Germans cracked down on bartering as they saw it as a way around the rationing system that encouraged the black market.

In these conditions, the black market thrived. People could buy scarce luxuries if they were prepared to pay exorbitant prices and some black marketeers grew rich by exploiting other islander's needs. Tea and sugar were always in demand but most sought-after was tobacco, and that often came from trading with German soldiers. Other goods

(top left)
Ausweis, a permit to travel.

(above)
'Make do and mend' bellows and toy boat.

(left)
Guernsey one penny and half penny stamps postmarked 21st December 1943.

were smuggled in from France by troops and sailors and some officers made profits on the side. It was of course illegal and the number of prosecutions of both civilians and Germans rose steadily through the war. Although 'black marketeers' were unpopular, the truth was that most islanders were driven into illicit dealing to some extent.

Residents who had received their income from savings or pensions in England had none. Some shops had closed and some businesses collapsed, so unemployment was initially high, as was under-employment. The Controlling Committee looked for jobs for people to do. Few wanted to work for the Germans, who started bringing in French labour on their engineering projects, but later in the Occupation their demands for labour left the island short of people with agricultural skills.

Boredom was the big enemy. There was a curfew at night and access to beaches and cliffs was restricted. Once the radios were confiscated, there was little to do at night. The cinemas soon ran out of English language films and only had German offerings which were largely aimed at the troops and laden with propaganda. Military bands would play in Candie Gardens but there was little enthusiasm when dances were organised. There was a growth in amateur dramatics, which kept the audiences amused, the performers occupied and challenged the ingenuity of dressmakers and set designers. Sport was permitted, but later

discouraged so people could save their energy. All this time islanders tried to make sense of the progress of the war through a fog of highly massaged 'news' put into the newspapers by the Germans and the whispers of hope from those who still listened to the BBC in secret. Everyone knew their lives were in the power of the enemy, every day.

(top)
Charm bracelet made post-war by Dorothy Higgs who lived through the Occupation.

(above)
Home-made wooden Wellington bomber model.

Frank Le Page

Festung Guernsey

Although the British had decided the Channel Islands had no strategic value and any attempt at defending them would be a waste of resources, the Germans took the opposite view. Capturing British territory had great propaganda value, and Hitler would prevent their recapture at all costs. The cost was enormous.

After the war the islands would not be returned to Britain, and the Nazis considered using them as a 'Strength Through Joy' tourist destination or a naval base. However, by 1941, Hitler's fear was that the British would try to retake the islands to distract German forces fighting in Greece, or to take advantage of the German attack on Russia. They were

to be made impregnable fortresses. The unspoken truth was that there was going to be no quick victory and by the end of 1941 Germany was on the defensive in the west.

319 Infantry Division was assigned to the islands for the rest of the war. Up to 37,000 soldiers with artillery, flak guns, aircraft, ships and tanks garrisoned the islands by the middle of 1942. 54,000 mines were laid in Guernsey, over 30,000 in Alderney and even 5,400 in Sark. Engineers ringed Guernsey with concrete bunkers, trenches, towers and artillery positions. Old Russian guns which had a range of 50km were installed in Batterie Mirus, which took a year and a half to complete.

(left)
A massive Russian naval gun being transported to install at Batterie Mirus.

German Anti-Aircraft (flak) positions at Clarence Battery, Fort George, 1944.

23

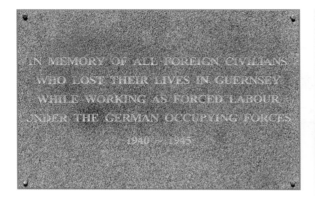

German *Feldmarschall* Von Rundstedt saw the folly of all this effort but could not defy Hitler's orders. He doubted the islands would ever be attacked, knew they had no value to Germany's war effort and he badly needed these men and resources to defend the French beaches where the real threat of invasion would come. Close to half a million tonnes of concrete was used. It is thought that 10% of the materials used in the *Atlantikwall* chain of fortifications were expended in the Channel Islands.

Civilian workers from the 'Organisation Todt' (OT) initially worked on these fortifications but more men were soon needed. Conscript labourers from occupied Europe were brought in, including Jews, political prisoners, forced and slave labourers from eastern Europe. Up to 7,000 came to Guernsey. In theory many were 'volunteers' and supposed to be paid but were cheated of both money and food. Some classes of

workers fared better than others, with the eastern European slave labourers especially being ill-treated, beaten by brutal guards and worked constantly. Up to 108 foreign workers are known to have died and were buried in Guernsey.

Slave workers tunnelled into the granite to create ammunition, fuel stores and ultimately the 'Underground Hospital' in St Andrews. A light railway was constructed running from St Peter Port around the coast as far as Perelle to carry construction materials.

By 1943 allied air attacks on shipping and French railways slowed the pace of construction and the size of the garrison also reduced. However, by July 1944 there were still 11,000 German personnel in Guernsey, around one for every two islanders. These fortifications were only briefly used in anger, as the Allies bypassed the islands when their liberation of France finally began.

(left)
Memorial to the Foreign Workers at St Peter Port Harbour.

(above)
German train running along the Esplanade loaded with cement.

(right)
Flak position (anti-aircraft gun) at Clarence Battery, Fort George.

(below)
Heavy artillery position. Batterie Elefant, St Andrew.

Deported

In late 1941, British forces interned German nationals in Iran and in retaliation Hitler demanded the deportation of 5,000 British-born Channel Islanders to the Pripet Marshes in Ukraine. Amid months of discussions and misunderstandings between the *Wehrmacht* and German Foreign Ministry, no action was taken. It was September 1942 before Hitler realised his order had not been carried out, and this time left his subordinates no option. The *Feldkommandatur* issued the orders, disregarding the protests of island officials and an announcement was made in

(above)
The internment camp at Biberach by J. S. Merry, 1943.

(left & below)
Biberach Camp.

The Star of September 15th. Men born outside the Island aged between 16 and 70 were singled out for deportation, together with their families and those whose permanent residence was not in the Channel Islands. In some cases only 12 hours' notice was given. Islanders were shocked by the order, some protested openly, and the deportees

were given a cheering send-off when they finally left on September 25th and 26th. A second, smaller batch of deportations were ordered in February 1943 in retaliation for a commando raid on Sark. It included men who had served in the British forces, British Jews, and those who had previously been imprisoned for acts of protest, defiance and resistance. Ambrose Sherwill and the husband of the Dame of Sark were amongst those on the list. An elderly English couple in Sark decided to commit suicide rather than be taken away, but the wife survived seriously injured. In total, 2,200 Channel Islanders were deported, with 1,003 from Guernsey and Sark.

(left)
Mr. W. R. Fletcher was deported to Dorsten - Stalag VI F/Z in September 1942.

(above)
Deportees in the train yard at Dorsten Transit Camp.

No special arrangements had been prepared to receive the deportees, amid the usual confusion between the various Nazi authorities. After some time spent at transit camps at Compiegne and Dorsten, families from Guernsey ended up principally interned at a former barracks near Biberach in southern Germany, with some at Schloss Wurzach, single men at Schloss Laufen plus a few at Liebenau. Camp captains were appointed, and the islanders set about surviving captivity as best they could. Conditions were primitive but deportees suffered none of the brutality seen in Germany's concentration camps and prisons. Military guards at Biberach were later replaced by police, mostly older men who developed cordial relationships with the islanders.

Food became a constant camp obsession, with standard fare being watery soup and tough rye bread supplemented by some fish, meat, potatoes and substitute coffee. In late 1942, deportees started to receive Red Cross parcels which enlivened the diet and boosted morale. Boredom was another challenge, and tempers often flared between the families cooped up together with no privacy. Ingenious deportees utilised whatever they could from Red Cross parcels – making baskets from the string, re-using wrapping as drawing paper or fashioning tin cans to make cups and utensils. Artwork produced by the deportees has been on display in Guernsey's museums and has even travelled back for exhibition in Biberach museum. The inclusion of red/white/blue, union flags or V-signs in art, greetings cards and clothing aimed at improving morale. Red Cross messages also allowed camp inmates to keep in contact with the islands.

Aluminium mug, engraved by Byll Balcombe at Biberach, 1943.

Tin candle holder, made from a butter tin by Mr P.J. Day while interned at Biberach.

School classes were organised, sports were popular, music and amateur dramatics helped fill the time. Art exhibitions were mounted, toys made for the children and corners of the camps turned into gardens. Regular walks in the countryside were permitted, people taking turns to join groups allowed out under guard. Getting out of the camp broke the boredom and offered the chance to gather firewood, pick apples and meet German civilians who would swap local produce for Red Cross items. Most people turned down the opportunity to do work outside the camps, but some ended up carrying out local jobs such as gardening in return for food.

The final winter of the war became difficult as the supply of Red Cross parcels and messages from home were cut off as the Allies advanced through France. Kept informed of the Allied victories by listening to concealed radios, the deportees knew that freedom was not far away. French troops liberated Biberach, Liebenau and Wurzach between 23 and 29 April 1944, with the Americans liberating Laufen on May 4th. Sixteen Guernsey people had died in these camps. Several children had been born and joined their parents returning home.

Greetings cards, badge and sampler made by deportees.

Child's toy made at Biberach camp.

Law and order

Guernsey's civil and criminal law continued to be enforced during the Occupation and the Royal Court continued to try cases as it had before. The island police operated in an uneasy relationship with German *Feldgendarmerie* and the *Geheime Feldpolizei*. Offences spotted by the German police, which disobeyed their orders were handled in the *Feldkommandant's* court; there were in addition courts set up by the Army, Navy and *Luftwaffe*. However, the infamous Gestapo did not operate in the islands except to sack the Freemasons' temple.

Guernsey's policemen were asked to stay in the islands and carry on at their posts when the German invasion was imminent, and most did so. Propaganda photographs of Guernsey 'bobbies' alongside German officers are amongst the strangest of the Occupation. None of the police spoke German or had the desire to learn, and they avoided saluting German officers whenever they could get away with it.

Crime had never been high in Guernsey, but wars bring out the worst in people. Theft became a major problem as soon as food began to run short. In 1944 there were almost 3,000 cases of food theft. There were infringements of the curfew and blackout rules to enforce, black marketeers to find and a steady stream of accidents in the unlit streets. Despite strict discipline German soldiers and Organisation Todt (OT) overseers were not subject to the curfew so were free to roam at night and farms were particularly vulnerable. A small number of locals who attempted to guard their property were assaulted or threatened with pistols or bayonets.

(above)
Guernsey Police Sergeant photographed by a German soldier in Market Street.

(right)
German Commandant Major Albrecht Lanz commandeered a Police car and required uniformed officers to drive it.

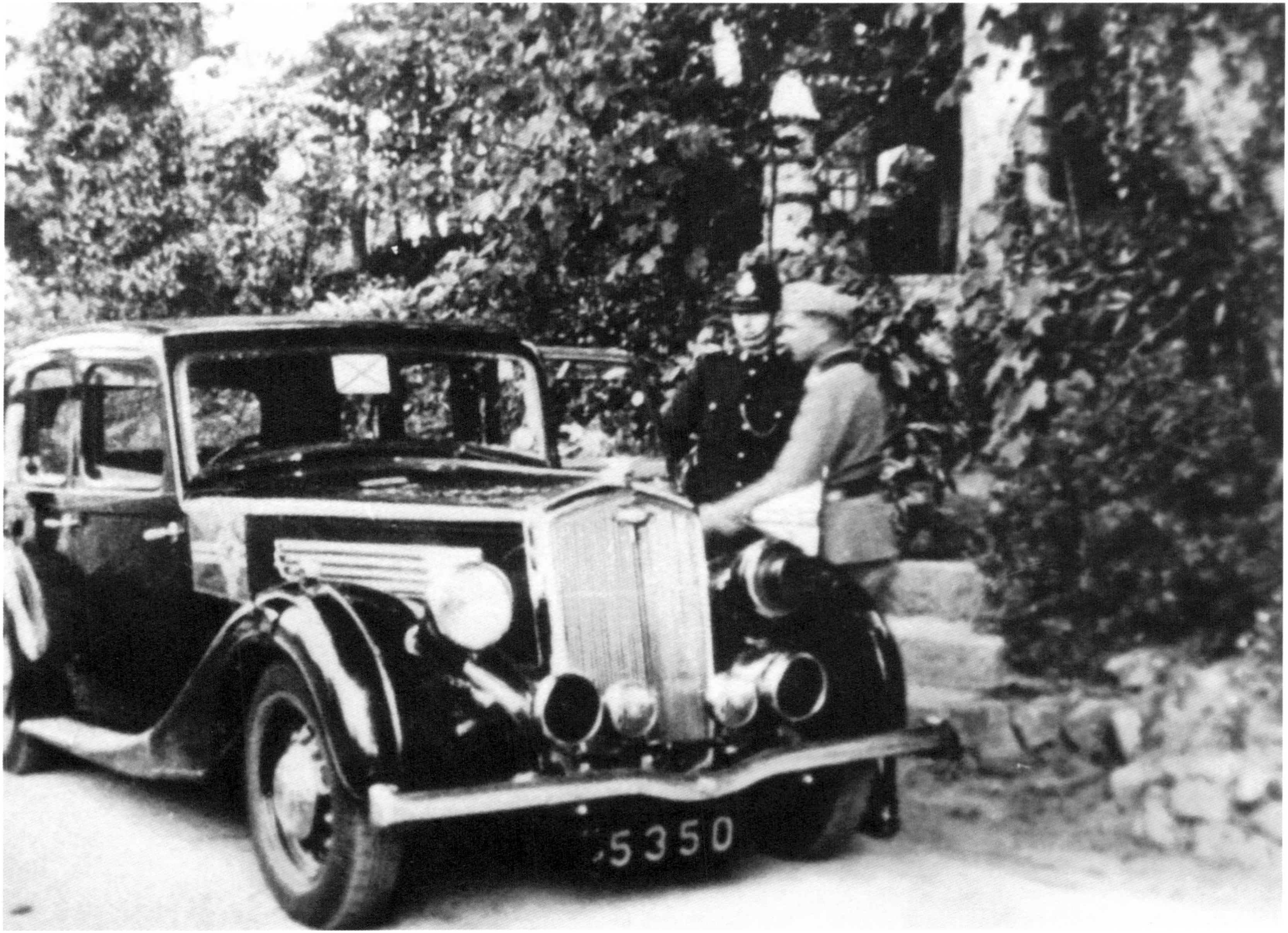
5350

Occupation Archive

Walther P38 pistol widely used by German forces.

Guernsey Police Sergeant Albert Lamy and civilian believed to be an interpreter with German soldiers in St James Street, possibly June 1940.

George Fisher was shot and killed by a drunken sergeant, Bertie Jehan was murdered whilst trying to stop theft of his potatoes and a German military policeman was also killed trying to protect a farm. The civilian policemen were thinly stretched and had difficulty bringing German troops to book. Indeed, they discouraged locals from making complaints against soldiers that could not be well verified. The German military police could be obstructive, and indifferent to minor offences, but murders, rapes and sexual assaults by soldiers and OT men were punished severely if the culprits were caught. Georgians serving with the Germans became particularly dangerous as discipline fell apart towards the end of the war.

Guernsey's authorities had the unpalatable task of enforcing Nazi regulations, including the Orders against the Jews, against which they did not protest. The customary formal language of letters between the Bailiff and the Inspector of Police makes for uncomfortable reading with the benefit of hindsight.

I have the honour to report that a total of four persons have registered as being of the Jewish persuasion"

Inspector Sculpher

Locals infringing wartime regulations might be fortunate to be caught by a Guernsey policeman rather than a German. A blind eye was sometimes turned, malicious tip-offs ignored, or a householder might be quietly warned if it became known they had a secret radio. Investigations into who had chalked anti-German V for victory signs were not always thorough, and indeed policemen themselves could be the culprits. The Postmaster also steamed open letters addressed to the *Feldkommandantur* and frequently 'lost' letters from informers.

The relationship between the police and the occupiers would ultimately suffer a tragic twist. Policemen were among few civilians permitted to move about after the curfew and at the end of 1941 started to carry out minor acts of sabotage to hit back at the occupiers. A pair of constables started Robin-Hood like raids on unguarded German stores, taking food to share with poorer families. Soon the majority of the force were involved in the theft of and giving away the loot, some of which came from stocks supposed to feed civilians or owned by civilians who were believed to be preferentially dealing with the Germans. German military police lay in wait in March 1942 and caught two constables red-handed. The whole force was arrested, their homes were searched and the men taken to the *Feldgendarmerie* headquarters at the Grange Lodge Hotel. Interrogated, beaten, and threatened with pistols, the men involved were forced to sign confessions. It was made clear that if they confessed they would be tried for civil crimes by the Royal Court, but if not they would be tried for sabotage by the German military and could be shot. Eighteen men were put on trial,

more than half the force. Three sergeants and 13 constables were sentenced to imprisonment, one sergeant acquitted, one constable won his appeal and another was released after serving a short sentence.

Inspector Sculpher was deported to Germany with his family in 1943, and Guernsey had to rebuild its police force almost from scratch. The sixteen former policemen were deported to France and then Germany, and split up almost randomly between various prisons, labour camps and concentration camps. Starved, ill and beaten, former PC Herbert Smith was murdered by a guard in Augsberg prison in April 1943. Although the others survived, most suffered from their injuries, camp diseases and Post Traumatic Stress Disorder for the rest of their lives.

Colonel Herbert Power, Chief Civil Affairs Officer, steps ashore at St Peter Port on 9th May, 1945. He is shaking hands with Inspector Albert Lamy, as Mr. Martel and Police Sergeant Bull look on.

Resistance & Repression

Across Occupied Europe, resistance groups fought back against the Germans and their allies, who punished local populations severely for acts of open defiance. Mass arrests, torture and execution of hostages were commonplace and whole villages were destroyed in retaliation for attacks by the resistance. An armed guerrilla war was out of the question in such a small place as Guernsey with no forests or mountains to hide in, where there was up to one soldier for every two islanders and the pick of young men had been evacuated. Guernsey's officials discouraged open defiance as they feared that the Germans would overreact.

Defiance in these conditions was limited to non-violent methods. It might be as subtle as deliberately misunderstanding German orders, tampering with a car or a waitress spitting in the soup. The fire brigade would take their time responding to a fire at a German establishment, and the grass at the airport would not be cut as short as the Luftwaffe required. Pranks such as changing road signs were punished by requiring local men to stand guard at the point for several nights. However, acts such as snipping telephone wires counted as sabotage and culprits risked being shot.

Trying to escape from the island was dangerous, but some brave souls succeeded. With their fear of spies, commando infiltration, air attacks and paratrooper landings plus 25,000 enemy civilians to control, the occupiers were always nervous. No Guernsey civilians were executed while still in the Island for acts of defiance, but arrest would be followed by rough interrogations, beatings or even torture. The lucky ones were imprisoned locally; the rest were shuttled around Nazi prisons, labour

(top)
Patriotic badge made by filing down a silver shilling. Made by Alf Williams.

(above)
Home-made crystal radio set.

camps and concentration camps in France, Germany or further afield where they were grossly maltreated, starved of good food, infected by lice, deprived of medicines and forced to do heavy manual work.

Inspired by a BBC broadcast in 1941, V for Victory signs began to appear all over Europe. In Guernsey they were often chalked, sometimes painted, on walls, roads or signs. The letter V was also worked into badges, clothing, embroideries and even stamp designs. It kept hope alive for those in the know. In some places the Germans adapted the V-sign by adding laurel leaves to graffiti that could not be easily removed. Sixty-year old French resident Xavier de Guillebon was sentenced to a year's imprisonment (of which he served 8 months) for chalking V-signs on the seats of German bicycles. As was often the case, someone had informed on him. Roy Machon was sentenced to five month's imprisonment for wearing a patriotic badge he had made.

After the Germans ordered all radio sets to be handed in permanently, those who dared keep their radios, or built crystal sets, continued to spread the news quietly. The Bailiff was kept well informed by his secretary, and also by an illicit news sheet which mysteriously started appearing on his desk.

The RAF occasionally dropped news sheets over the islands. The Germans forbade circulation of this 'propaganda'.

PROCLAMATION

1.

It is forbidden to circulate enemy propaganda material by hand or to spread the contents thereof.

2.

All enemy propaganda material found must be handed in immediately at the Feldkommandantur.

3.

Enemy propaganda material, in the sense of this proclamation, includes all publications which have not been issued or expressly authorized by the German Authorities.

4.

In so far as no other penal-law imposes a heavier sentence, contraventions of this proclamation shall be punished according to paragraph 4 of the Special Military Criminal-Law, of the 17th August, 1938, by a term of imprisonment not exceeding 15 years.

In particularly mild cases a fine may be imposed.

29th JULY, 1940.

Chief of the Military Administration Authorities for the North-West of France.

| Joseph Gillingham | Ernest Legg | Cecil Duquemin | Charles Machon | Frank Falla | Hubert Lanyon | Henrietta Gillingham |

Island Archives

From May 1942 the Guernsey Underground News Service (GUNS) was formed, based at the office of *The Star* newspaper. Six days a week, eight copies of a news sheet were typed on tomato packing paper and distributed to others to type and share more copies. The GUNS reporters drew their news by listening to the 9pm BBC broadcast on hidden radios, then worked into the night wary of Germans suddenly turning up at the office. GUNS continued until February 1944, but by that time copies were falling into careless hands and the team was betrayed by an Irish resident.

Charles Machon, Cecil Duquemin, Ernest Legg, Frank Falla, Joseph Gillingham and Hubert Lanyon were arrested, interrogated and sentenced to imprisonment. The men managed to protect other relatives and friends involved including Henrietta Gillingham. All the men except Lanyon were sent to France only days before D-Day. A red patch on their prison uniforms marked them out as 'politicial prisoners' and they would pay a high price for their defiance. Already unwell, Machon died in Hamelin in October 1944. After a year of hard labour, maltreatment and near-starvation Falla and Legg lay seriously ill in Naumberg prison when they were liberated by the Americans in April 1945. Neither would have survived many more weeks. Joseph Gillingham was said to have been released in February 1945, but it was not until 2016 that his family received confirmation that he had died in Halle Prison and was buried in the local cemetery in an area reserved for prisoners of the Nazis. Duquemin survived a series of forced labour camps and managed to briefly escape in Czechoslovakia during the confusion at the end of the war before being recaptured by the Russians.

The typewriter used by Frank Falla to produce uncensored news sheets can be seen at the German Occupation Museum, Guernsey.

Starving slave workers dressed in rags and driven brutally to work inspired compassion, especially among women. Food was short for everyone, but islanders would quietly pass a crust of bread or a vegetable into eager hands. Salvation Army Major Marie Ozanne and her family helped feed OT workers billeted near their Vale home and she dared write to the *Feldkommandantur* to protest about their treatment. She had already become a thorn in the side of the Germans for refusing orders not to wear her Salvation Army uniform. She also wrote a series of letters protesting against their treatment of the Jews. Her stark moral condemnation of the Nazis led to her arrest and imprisonment, although she was not mistreated and was released after six weeks. However, she was already ill and died shortly afterwards aged 37.

In the first year of the occupation, 20-year old John Ingrouille was accused by two women of organising a resistance army. Although a ludicrous charge, he was deported and imprisoned for the rest of the war and died of Tuberculosis shortly after being freed in Berlin by the Soviet Army in 1945. Englishman Percy Miller was convicted of owning a secret radio in 1943 and died in prison in Frankfurt little over a year later, possibly beaten to death. What in everyday terms might be viewed as crimes also became political. Aged 20, Sydney Ashcroft stole food from a German kitchen to feed his mother and ended up in a brawl with

soldiers. Moved from prison to prison, he died of TB in Straubing in April 1945.

Together with Louis Symes and policeman Herbert Smith, eight Guernsey civilians in total are recognised as having died due to standing up to the Nazis.

June 26th, 1941.

Dear Sir,
    Why do you persecute the Jews?
    Do you remember that they were God's chosen people, and that JESUS Himself was a Jew, the only ONE by whom we can inherit eternal life and enter heaven?
    If you think the Jews have done wrong, but have we not all sinned, and would it not be more profitable to them, to you, and to us all if we tried to save their souls instead of oppressing their minds and bodies? We would then at least be laying up treasure in heaven. "And with God there is no respect of persons, but in every nation he that feareth Him and worketh righteousness is accepted of Him."
    Believe me, Sir, I pray for your highest good, and for the good of those you love.
            Yours sincerely,
            (Marie Ozanne)

Marie Ozanne, and transcript of a letter she wrote condemning German behaviour. A blue plaque has been erected at her home in the Vale.

GUERNSEY MUSEUMS
Major
Marie Ozanne O.F.
Salvation Army
1906 – 1943
a resister to oppression
lived here

Under the Jackboot

For all the veneer of behaving in a civilised manner during the Occupation, ultimately the Nazis showed their true colours. Most Channel Island Jews made sure they were evacuated before the invasion. Those who remained, most of whom had come to the island to escape Nazism in their own countries, were subject to an increasingly repressive series of 'Orders'. The way in which island authorities followed these orders remains a sensitive subject to this day. Although the true horror of the Holocaust had not been discovered by the world, the destruction of Jewish property, ill-treatment and internment of Jews in concentration camps following *Kristallnacht* in November 1938 was well known and reported at the time in the Channel Islands. President of the Controlling Committee, Ambrose Sherwill, later admitted "...I still feel ashamed that I did not do something by way of protest to the Germans..."

The 'Order Relating to Measures against the Jews' registered by the Royal Court on 23 October 1940 was the first of a series of increasingly repressive measures. In March 1941, the registration cards of all Jews had to be marked with a red J. Perhaps Guernsey's officials could have protested or resigned, but to ensure local complicity in what followed the Germans required the Orders made into local law rather than remaining purely Nazi directives.

Therese Steiner was working as a nanny in Sark when war broke out and was at first detained as an 'enemy alien' as she had been born in Austria. Cook Auguste Spitz was also Austrian, and also initially interned. After the German invasion, both women were released and found work at the Castel Hospital and both registered as Jews in 1940 as the First Order required. However Polish

horticulture worker Marianne Grunfeld hid
her Jewish origins until she was uncovered
in 1942, possibly due to an informant if not
simply due to her name arousing suspicion.
All three women were arrested in April
1942 and ordered to be deported. Appeals
were made by Grunfeld's employer but she,
Steiner and Spitz were deported to France
and lodged initially with nuns. In June they
were forced to wear the yellow star, and in
July they were rounded up with other Jews
and put on trains bound for the Auschwitz-
Birkenau concentration camp. All three
were murdered there.

Fate and the fine print of Nazi bureaucracy
allowed others to survive. Elda Brouard
(née Bauer) and Elizabet Duquemin (née
Fink) had married British men. As British
Jews they were among the group deported
in 1943 joining those held at Biberach.
Czech-born Annie Wranowsky who held a
German passport worked as a housekeeper
in Sark and was officially identified as a
Jew, with a red J added to her identity
card. She was ordered to be deported in
1942, but somehow managed to argue
she had Aryan ancestry so was allowed
to remain in Sark for the rest of the war.
Miriam Jay was the partner of Advocate
George Ridgeway. Ironically, he helped
draft four of the nine anti-Jewish Orders
before his death in 1942 but risked a great
deal to help conceal her Jewish ancestry.
No-one betrayed her, and Jay survived
undetected for the whole war.

Therese Steiner

Auguste Spitz

Marianne Grunfeld

Island Archives

Memorial to the three
Jewish women at
St Peter Port Harbour.

(left)
Organisation Todt men celebrate Christmas in the islands. Tableware and cutlery could be stamped with the Nazi eagle.

(below)
Soldiers pose by the door of their billet.

The Occupiers

Islanders made a distinction between the fanatical Nazis they encountered, the polite old-fashioned officer class and those ordinary soldiers who had not lost their humanity. With the war in Russia consuming thousands of lives the toughest men were needed at the front. Soldiers sent to the islands were often older men, some veterans of the Great War, and those made less fit by wounds. Young men might chafe for action, but others were simply happy to be away from the fighting.

"It would be unjust not to admit that the German rule to which we were subjected was on the whole mild and the behaviour of most individual Germans was good" (Ralph Durand).

The worst were arrogant, including officers who took over the best houses and treated them and their contents as personal property.

Furniture, art and cars were shipped home. Friendlier officers were baffled by islander's reluctance to socialise with them, as they expected to be welcomed into polite society, not understanding that loyal Guernsey people continued to regard them as the enemy.

Despite Guernsey's charms, a major problem for soldiers of all eras is boredom. Some resorted to drinking, and drunkenness was behind the majority of cases of assaults and criminal damage inflicted on islanders. More constructive use of their time was made by those of an artistic nature, creating works that still endure. Several bunkers are decorated

(above)
Soldiers queue for food.

(right)
An officer strikes a nonchalant pose.

Both photographs taken by Georg Späth, a German soldier, in 1942.

with murals and precisely executed texts in gothic script, some with Nazi symbolism but others simply there to be appreciated. Carved wooden mementoes and paintings of local scenes were used to decorate bunkers and billets, were sent home to their families, presented to comrades or given to their unwilling Guernsey hosts.

Accidents were a major cause of death amongst the Germans, involving vehicles, landmines and other ordnance. Pinprick attacks by the RAF and Royal Navy extracted a toll, men were driven by despair to suicide and soldiers were shot for committing serious crimes. The military cemetery at Fort George includes 111 German graves from the Second World War, although other casualties were taken to France. Some 70 initially buried in Alderney included seven suicides and two shot by firing squad; these were exhumed after the war and reburied in a military cemetery in France.

319 Division was fortunate to see no fighting beyond the occasional air-raid or shelling by the Royal Navy. Guernsey and Sark were (food scarcity aside) pleasant places to be posted and a good many soldiers developed

an affection for the islands. Some even returned after the war to be reunited with locals they had grown to know or revisit beauty spots. The former commander of the German Naval Signals HQ at St Jacques came to support its restoration. With the passage of time, the bad taste left by the war faded and a steady stream of German visitors continue to come to the Occupation sites, including the children and grandchildren of the occupiers.

Soldiers line up in a typical Guernsey 'vinery'.

(right)
Letter opener carved by a German soldier.

(left)
Field telephones
in action, Festung
Guernsey.

(top and right)
German films were
shown at Guernsey
cinemas whilst
soldiers would
amuse themselves
by making works of
art or carving.

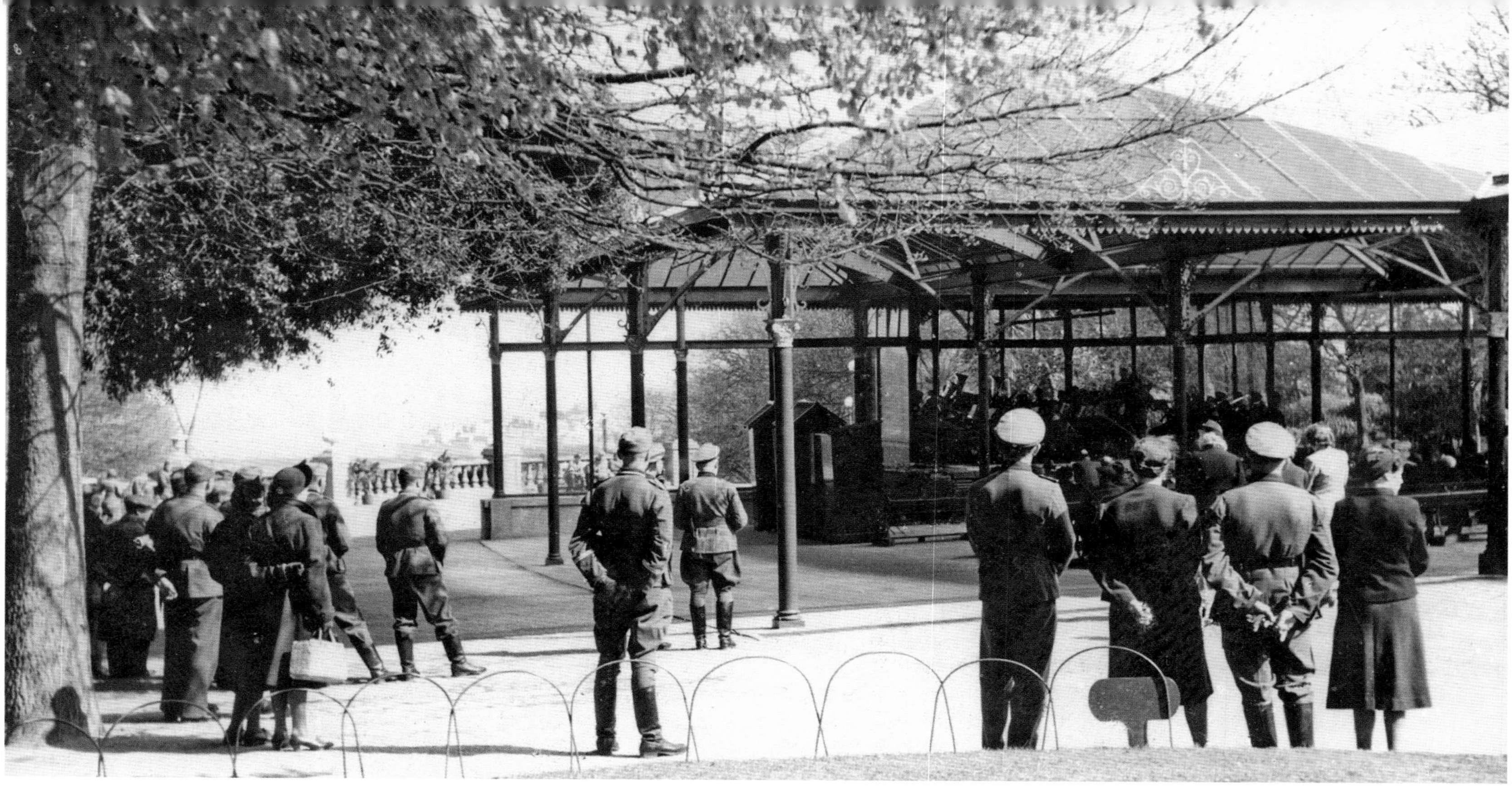

My Enemy is My Friend

After the war some British newspapers criticised the behaviour of Channel Islanders during the Occupation. The Germans wanted islanders to work for them, and they argued with the Controlling Committee over what counted as 'war work', as The Hague Convention in theory protected civilians from being forced to work on military projects.

To get around this the occupier offered high wages and extra food to anyone who chose to work for them. In reality a majority of the people on the island worked with the Germans in one way or another, from the shop assistant serving soldiers with her regular customers, to the grower whose tomatoes were eaten by the occupiers.

(above)
Civilian women mingle with German officers at a band concert in Candie Gardens.

(right)
Nutcracker carved by a German soldier.

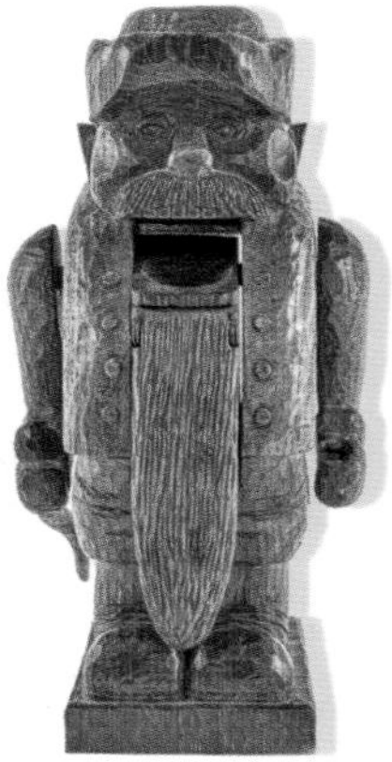

A small number of residents were happy to 'collaborate' - that is co-operate openly with the Germans, including some Irish workers who felt no love for Britain due to their Republican sympathies. Some self-justification came from a sense that the islands had been abandoned, even betrayed by Britain. Memoirs written by islanders are bitter about the small percentage who collaborated with too much enthusiasm, those who made money from the black market and especially those who betrayed their neighbours.

Tony Hobbs was only a boy when his father was killed on the lifeboat during the German air attack, yet he has photographs of his family posing with soldiers and tells how one of them even gave him toy soldiers.

Soldiers were billeted on Guernsey families, and though some behaved arrogantly, others treated their hosts with respect and friendships

Occupation banknotes

Tony Hobbs as a child with German soldiers.

developed. They missed their own families and their homes, particularly as the tide of war turned and the Royal Air Force (RAF) started to destroy German cities. Far from home it was inevitable that German soldiers would be attracted to local women, and teenage girls were growing up in islands crowded by smartly dressed young men. Some fell in love, but others were taken advantage of, or simply made the best of the moment. The promise of extra food, cigarettes and alcohol drew some women into relationships, and officers were particularly good catches for a woman who did not care for her reputation. Women who dated Germans were derided as 'Jerrybags', and it remains a sensitive subject even now. It aroused great anger at the time, controversy after the war and claims that hundreds of illegitimate children were born to German fathers, although the true number is probably less than 100. Genuine love affairs flourished and endured; after his release from a Prisoner of War (PoW) camp at the end of the war, medic Werner Rang was one who married his island sweetheart.

It is easy to pass judgement from the comfort of modern times, knowing how the war would end. Those who informed on neighbours, sometimes leading to their deaths, cannot be excused for their actions but the large majority of islanders simply tried to get on with daily life. At the time, few expected the war to last so long, and successive German victories up to 1941 even made it look like they were going to win. As the Occupation dragged on, 'daily life' became a struggle to survive.

The five McGrath sisters were evacuated in 1940 and rather than be split up, decided to all join the Auxiliary Territorial Service (ATS).

Guernsey Strikes Back

Any impression that Channel Islanders simply sat out the war is belied by the war memorials in each island and parish. It is estimated that between 8,000 and 10,000 men and women from Guernsey, Alderney and Sark served in the British forces during the war and 'did their bit' to defeat the Axis powers; close to a quarter of the pre-war population. 223 gave their lives and more were wounded, saved from sinking ships, bailed out of stricken aircraft or were taken prisoner. Guernseymen were evacuated from Dunkirk, landed on D-Day, at Salerno and Arnhem, and crossed the Rhine. They fought in deserts, the jungles, the Arctic, the skies, and across the oceans, some not returning for months or indeed years after the liberation. Carel Toms was trapped with the British Expeditionary Force (BEF) in 1940 and spent his war in a PoW camp, Herbert Pike fought with partisans in Italy, and evacuee Herbert Mauger volunteered to serve in midget submarines in the Far East. Sergeant Henry Hamon and Lieutenant R Ferbrache had the pleasure of being in the advance party of Force 135 that came ashore on Liberation Day.

Herbert Machon and his Spitfire XVI 'Guernsey's Reply'.

Air Chief Marshal Sir Peter de Lacey Le Cheminant GBE KCB DFC

Graham Jackson

In December 1943, at the age of 26, Herbert Le Patourel was acting Major in the Hampshire Regiment. During the defence of Terbourba in Tunisia, German troops took the high ground and needed to be dislodged. Le Patourel led four volunteers to silence a number of machine-gun positions, and when all the other men had fallen casualties he continued alone, armed with a pistol and grenades. As he did not return, he was presumed killed and was awarded the Victoria Cross (VC) 'posthumously' for his gallantry. Only later was it discovered that he had in fact been badly wounded and captured. He was repatriated from an Italian hospital and received his VC in 1943, recovering sufficiently to take part in the campaigns to liberate Europe in 1944-45.

Peter Le Cheminant graduated from RAF Cranwell as a pilot in 1939, aged 19. By the age of 22 he was an acting Wing Commander. In May 1942 he took part in two of the three Thousand Bomber raids over Germany and a few weeks later flew on the ill-fated Allied raid on Dieppe. In late 1942 he left for North Africa leading bombers supporting British troops in North Africa, Sicily and Italy, and was awarded the Distinguished Flying Cross. By the end of 1943 he had completed 83 often hazardous operations and returned to England to plan for attacks against Japan. After a long career in the RAF, including flying in the Korean War, he was appointed Lieutenant-Governor of Guernsey from 1980 to 1985 and was the first native Guernseyman to hold this post for 600 years. He died in 2018 aged 97.

Women also played their part in the victory. Elizabeth Martel, later Lady Frossard, was a Wren in the Royal Navy on signals duty. Women's Auxiliary Air Force member Joan Thomas worked on air reconnaissance photographs, including those taken of the Channel Islands. Kathleen Falla was evacuated with the Ladies' College girls and in 1942 joined the Wrens, assigned to 'Special Duties PV' the allied code-breaking operation. It was top secret and gruelling work in heavily restricted areas, which she couldn't talk about or hope for a transfer until the war ended.

The Evacuees

"THE STAR," WEDNESDAY, JUNE 19, 1940. GUERNSEY'S OLDEST NEWSPAPER ESTABLISHED 1813

The Star

"THE STAR" may be posted to Canada and Newfoundland at magazine rates. Registered at the G.P.O. as a newspaper.

CXXVI.—No. 146 WEDNESDAY, JUNE 19, 1940. GRATIS

ISLAND EVACUATION
ALL CHILDREN TO BE SENT TO MAINLAND TOMORROW

Mothers May Accompany Those Under School Age

REGISTRATION TONIGHT
WHOLE BAILIWICK TO BE DEMILITARISED

Strong Advice To Men Between 20 and 33

Compared to the chaos which led up to the Evacuation in June 1940, the arrival of Channel Islanders in England was well organised. Britain already had a plan for mass evacuation of cities and this experience helped the smooth reception and transport of some 25,000 refugees arriving on over 40 ships. The Islanders landed at Weymouth as refugees with no homes, no jobs, and only the possessions they could carry. Children wore luggage tags tied to their clothing bearing their names and carried gas masks in cardboard boxes. Some travelled on alone armed simply with the name of a relative who would meet them at a distant station. Trains carried their human cargo north to safety in the towns of Cheshire, Lancashire and West Yorkshire. Accommodation was found at first in town halls, empty buildings and with families with space to spare.

The industrial towns were a stark contrast to 'home' and islanders and northerners struggled with each other's accents. Snow was a unique experience, especially for

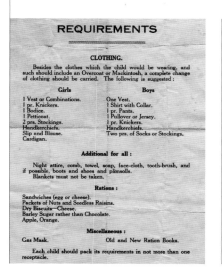

REQUIREMENTS

CLOTHING.

Besides the clothes which the child would be wearing, and such should include an Overcoat or Mackintosh, a complete change of clothing should be carried. The following is suggested :

Girls	Boys
1 Vest or Combinations.	One Vest.
1 pr. Knickers.	1 Shirt with Collar.
1 Bodice.	1 pr. Pants.
1 Petticoat.	1 Pullover or Jersey.
2 prs. Stockings.	1 pr. Knickers.
Handkerchiefs.	Two prs. of Socks or Stockings.
Slip and Blouse.	
Cardigan.	

Additional for all :

Night attire, comb, towel, soap, face-cloth, tooth-brush, and if possible, boots and shoes and plimsolls.
Blankets must not be taken.

Rations :

Sandwiches (egg or cheese).
Packets of Nuts and Seedless Raisins.
Dry Biscuits—Cheese.
Barley Sugar rather than Chocolate.
Apple, Orange.

Miscellaneous :

Gas Mask. Old and New Ration Books.

Each child should pack its requirements in not more than one receptacle.

the children. After the initial dispersal, the refugees began to spread back to London and the south coast by choice, or to stay with relatives and many ended up in Glasgow. Men and women sought jobs, which for some came easier than others. The fortunate managed to settle, but others moved from home to home, job to job, especially as the Germans began to bomb the cities, and what seemed like a haven became no longer safe. The Dame of Sark's son was killed in an air raid on Liverpool in 1941 whilst on leave, and a V1 flying bomb interrupted a meeting of the Kent Channel Islands Society whose members fortunately escaped harm.

(above)
Evacuees' Christmas party in Portsmouth, 1943.

(left)
The *Isle of Sark* with evacuees leaving Guernsey bound for the UK, 1940.

Toy dog made for an evacuee, Hugh Lenfestey.

The Ladies College girls and the Elizabeth College boys travelled with their teachers to Oldham, where many were soon collected by the parents who had managed to escape Guernsey. The remaining 'Ladies' were relocated to a public school in Denbigh, whilst the 'Elizabethans' went to spartan camps in the Peak District, which opened up new adventures for the boys. The Castel school went to Bury, the Intermediate school girls merged with a school in Rochdale, and the boys with one in Oldham. When children attained adulthood, they could of course sign up with the British forces and join the fight back.

A Channel Islands Refugee Committee was formed and received donations in cash from expatriate islanders already living in England. Based in London it collected clothes and took in requests for assistance from the refugees. Appeals were made on the BBC, and collections were made at meetings and speaking engagements organised by islanders across the country. Local societies sprang up where there were concentrations of Channel Islanders, organising social events, relief efforts and publishing news. Even a lodge of Freemasons was established in London. The Guernsey Society was formed by Sir Donald Banks in 1943, and is still an active society for expatriates, publishing its Review 75 years later.

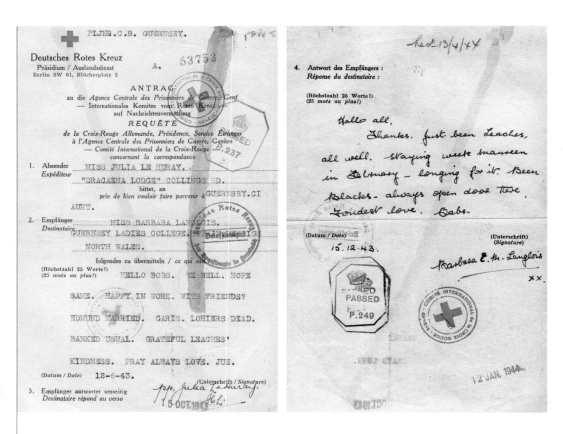

Red Cross Messages

Communication with family and friends back in the islands was at first impossible, then, after much behind-the-scenes negotiation, it became possible to send messages via the Red Cross from the end of 1940. A Red Cross message was limited to 25 words and was censored by both the British and German authorities, as well as inspected by the Red Cross in Geneva. It travelled to the islands via Portugal, France and Switzerland

Evacuees on their way home at last, Crewe, 1945.

and could take six months to arrive. The sender had to choose their words thoughtfully, but subtly coded messages could be incorporated to evade the censors. By late 1941 the Germans allowed islanders to send one message a month back in reply, and the latest news was often shared around meetings of refugees. Hints from the islands might indicate they were short of food, the radios or the family car had been confiscated and in return the evacuees might refer to fictional characters doing well by way of sharing war news.

'Adolf' Island

Only 1436 people lived in Alderney in 1940, and almost all of them chose to be evacuated on six ships which departed for Weymouth on June 23rd. Boats were sent from Guernsey to rescue 400 cattle and other farm animals that had been abandoned, plus medical supplies. Later runs organised the lifting of the potato crop and the recovery of equipment. Some of the remaining islanders were persuaded to leave but seven stubbornly stayed put.

The German garrison of Alderney was initially small, and plans were made to improve agriculture to help feed Guernsey. Work parties were brought over from Guernsey to work the land and assist in extending the harbour at Braye. Alderney's empty houses and shops were looted and left ransacked. What part was played in this by the Germans, by French refugees and sailors or by the Guernsey work parties will never be known, but an Englishman from Guernsey was amongst a group prosecuted by the Germans in a well-publicised effort to discourage looting.

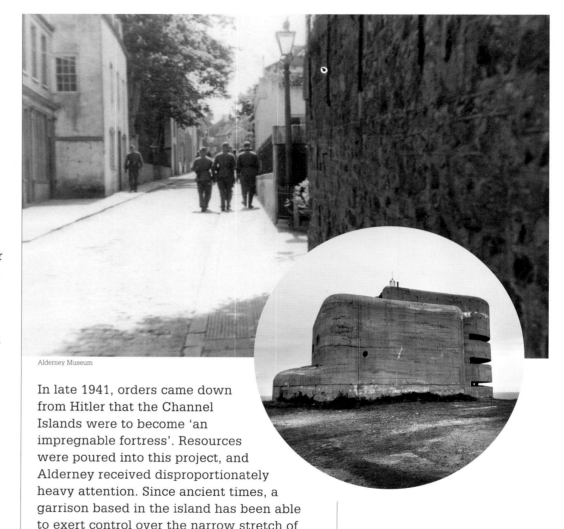

Alderney Museum

In late 1941, orders came down from Hitler that the Channel Islands were to become 'an impregnable fortress'. Resources were poured into this project, and Alderney received disproportionately heavy attention. Since ancient times, a garrison based in the island has been able to exert control over the narrow stretch of water between the east coast and France, and the Germans even took over the old Roman fort at the Nunnery and re-fortified it as Resistance Point *Piratenschloss*. Massive fortifications included anti-tank walls, five

(top)
Occupied Alderney.

(above)
Rangefinding and Observation tower known as 'the Odeon'.

coastal artillery batteries, and numerous flak, anti-tank and machine-gun bunkers. The extensive forts built by the British in the 19th century were modified for modern times and a prominent artillery rangefinding and observation tower constructed.

By late 1942 the Guernsey workers had been withdrawn and the island was totally militarised, with up to 3,200 German troops stationed there. A few officers brought their girlfriends, a small number of French prostitutes were brought over and some women were employed in support functions such as catering but the population was overwhelmingly male. Soldiers quickly became bored with the isolated island devoid of all normal life. Troops from other islands were even posted to Alderney as a punishment.

Building the fortifications fell to the Organisation Todt, whose codename for Alderney was 'Adolf'. From July 1942, shiploads of OT slave workers began arriving, reaching a maximum estimated at 4,000. The 'volunteers' were predominantly east Europeans referred to as 'Russians' but including Poles and Ukrainians, plus Frenchmen and some Moroccan prisoners of war amongst 27 nationalities.

Workers were based in four camps named Helgoland, Norderney, Borkum and Sylt, although a fifth camp named Citadella has also been alleged. Sylt became a

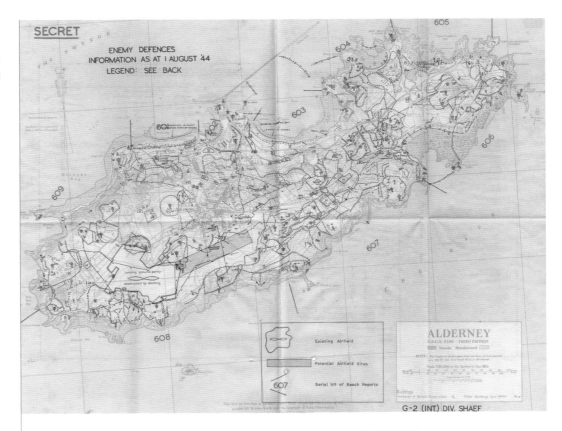

Alderney Museum

(above)
British map of 1944 showing German fortifications in Alderney.

(left)
The fortifications under construction.

Alderney Museum

Alderney Museum

The Organisation
Todt constructing the
fortifications of Alderney.

concentration camp run by the *Schutzstaffel* (SS) for around 500 political prisoners, including Jews, Spanish republicans and German dissidents. Men were worked with barely a break and wore the clothes they arrived in until they became rags. In theory the workers were to receive rations on an agreed scale, but German military personnel and OT officers systematically diverted the food and sold it off. The workers were badly fed on a diet of watery soup, substitute coffee and hunks of stale bread. Any pay the men were supposed to receive was stolen, and Red Cross parcels due to prisoners of war were sold off. The Germans punished some of the culprits for theft and corruption, but none for the suffering they inflicted. OT Guards and 'trusted' prisoners set up as overseers were encouraged to be brutal. Sticks, rubber hoses filled with sand and leather whips were used liberally. Men would be beaten for many reasons, particularly for

German *Reichsarbeitsdienst* (National Labour Service) belt buckle.

grabbing extra food – even rotten vegetables, scraps from the garbage or animal innards buried by the slaughterhouse. These were not extermination camps, but men died of exhaustion and heavy beatings, some are reported to have been shot out of hand and some hanged as punishments. Escape was of course impossible. The beautiful holiday island of Alderney became a place of suffering, inhumanity, degradation and death.

The Organisation Todt constructing the fortifications of Alderney.

At least 389 slave workers died in Alderney, based on Germans' own records and immediate post-war investigations.
The number is widely thought to have been higher, although not the thousands of deaths by execution claimed by some more ghoulish accounts. Most workers were withdrawn from the island in mid-1944 but surviving Alderney did not mean they would survive the war. Ships and trains took them to work on V1 sites in France, but ultimately the fate of too many was to be murdered in concentration camps, from which many had been initially brought to the Island.

The Hammond Memorial remembers the men of many nations who died due to Nazi brutality in Alderney.

Alderney Museum

War Comes to the Islands

The major battlefronts of the war were distant, but the British did not let the Germans occupy the islands in peace. During the Battle of Britain in 1940, British aircraft attacked Guernsey airport which was being used by the *Luftwaffe*. Air actions took place over the islands throughout the war, with 153 Allied aircrew known to have died and others taken prisoner. Planes that crashed near the islands were often already damaged and heading for home.

Hit-and-run raids lasting only a few seconds were made against the harbour, radar positions and other military targets by the RAF. A Guernsey crane operator was killed in one raid, but the main danger to islanders came from the shrapnel from German anti-aircraft fire dropping back to earth. Activity was particularly heavy in 1944 when planes supporting the Normandy campaign passed close to the islands, and George Malbon was killed by a falling German A-A shell on D-Day. Jittery German gunners even shot down a couple of their own planes.

As the tide of war started to turn in favour of the Allies, the RAF was active in attacking shipping by daylight, whilst Royal Navy destroyers and torpedo boats prowled the seas at night. Shipwrecks in the waters between the islands and the French mainland testify to their success, but also to the failures. In October 1943, the cruiser HMS *Charybdis* and the Destroyer HMS *Limbourne* were sunk by enemy E-boats in a disastrous

Guernsey Press

Bell from the sixth ship named HMS *Charybdis*, 1969. The bell rope was made by a survivor of the 1943 attack. Used annually at the memorial service.

Guernsey Press

night action west of Jersey. 21 bodies washed up in Guernsey, one in Sark and 29 in Jersey. In Guernsey the authorities allowed the men to have a military funeral at the Foulon cemetery and were taken off guard when a third of the population turned out in a massive show of patriotism. The event is still commemorated as 'Charybdis Day'.

For all the sense of being forgotten, Channel Islanders were fortunate that the Allies did not carry out the plans they drafted to recapture the islands. Lord Mountbatten planned an invasion of Guernsey by troops landing at L'Ancresse after massed bombers had 'softened up' the north of the island. The loss of life, both military and civilian, would have been enormous, and the Allies realised there would be little benefit for such a cost. Alderney was also the objective of cancelled landings planned on equally devastating scale.

(below)
Flight Lt Saville of the Royal Canadian Air Force was shot down in Havelet Bay whilst attacking German radars on 5 June 1940.

Plenty of smaller raids were also cancelled, which was a relief for the islanders who would have suffered reprisals as the price for any success. A few went ahead and in September 1942 the small-scale raid 'Dryad' captured the 7-man crew of the Casquets lighthouse off Alderney. 'Basalt' was a Commando landing on Sark the following month to gather intelligence and the news even reached the desk of Hitler. Four Germans were killed and one captured. The raid, coupled with that in Dieppe, had unexpected repercussions including allied PoWs being shackled amid a diplomatic row over the treatment of prisoners. It provoked a second round of deportations and encouraged Hitler's infamous 'Commando Order', where captured commandos were to be shot. A further operation against Sark in 1943, 'Hardtack 7', failed when two raiders were killed by mines.

By 1944 the British came around to the objective of retaking the islands without a shot being fired, working first towards encouraging the garrison to surrender, then simply waiting for the war to end if they did not. The new plan would be called 'Operation Nestegg', and 'Omelette' was the name given to the initial landings which might have to face resistance from die-hard Germans. Force 135 was formed to carry it out.

Siege

D-Day, 6th of June 1944, is the date the Nazi grip on Western Europe started its final decline. Allied troops landed on the beaches of Normandy, breaking through the *Atlantikwall* that would have been much stronger without the material wasted fortifying the islands. Hungry, cold, bored and repressed islanders waited for their turn to be liberated, or for the German commanders to simply throw in the towel. When D-Day came it was not the end of their troubles, but the start of the Occupation's most desperate chapter.

Von Schmettow wanted to send his troops to join the fight in Normandy. It made no military sense for the Germans to hang on to the islands, but Hitler ordered his prize pieces of British territory to be defended to the last bullet. The OT workers and some German support troops were evacuated to France. The SS were pulled out of Alderney to prevent them being captured however a whole reinforced division of troops was left cut off in the islands and lost to the German war effort. Disillusioned soldiers began to call themselves 'The Canada Division', knowing they would end up in a Prisoner of War camp. Belief in victory was replaced by resolve to 'hold on to the last'.

Carel Toms

The Americans captured Cherbourg by the end of June and St Malo in August. Occupiers and Occupied were now equally trapped. The supply of food, coal and medicines by sea almost ceased. Only an occasional aircraft would make it through carrying mail or supplies. Crime increased as the discipline of the German troops and East European auxiliaries began to break down. Soldiers were ordered to start growing vegetables and potatoes and go fishing. By October, medicines had run out and the Germans estimated that no food would be left by January 1945. However, if the civilian rations were reduced to just vegetables, the garrison might hold out for another year.

Evacuating the civilians or letting them starve would weaken the defence as three quarters of them were doing essential work, and only some of this could be taken over by the troops. Even at

(left)
Women collecting Red Cross Parcels.

(below)
Bottles preserving carrageen moss which was eaten in desperation and coffee substitute made from corn.

this stage of the war the British and Germans carried on a diplomatic argument over whose responsibility it was to feed the islanders and tried to score propaganda points. Winston Churchill and his ministers discussed proposals to evacuate the civilians or send them food, but these were rejected, and Churchill infamously wrote 'let them starve!'. He meant the Germans, but by the winter of 1944, the civilians were starving too. People were even eating seaweed.

The Bailiff of Guernsey complained of the shortages to Von Schmettow and was finally allowed to contact the Red Cross. The Controlling Committee meantime took matters into their own hands and wrote a report on the dire situation which they entrusted to mariner Fred Noyon, who escaped by boat on November 3rd. Unbeknown to them, the British had by this time decided to send food parcels. More arguments delayed the departure of the Red Cross ship SS *Vega* which did not arrive in St Peter Port until December 27th. It carried 100,000 food parcels from Canada and New Zealand plus medicines and supplies including salt, soap and tobacco.

Red Cross Parcels delivered to St Peter Port harbour by the SS *Vega*.

The arrival of *Vega* saved Guernsey from starvation, but as the Red Cross were now effectively feeding the civilians it meant the troops had enough food to last out the war.

In January the Germans launched raids to confiscate food from any civilian who still had 'excessive' stocks and were surprised by how much they found. Troops were to avoid long spells of duty to save energy. By this time the civilian diet was little more than 1,100 calories per day compared to 3,500 in Britain. The meat ration was down to 4 ounces per person every three weeks.

Von Schmettow refused Allied demands to surrender, but he was recalled in February 1945 and replaced by his deputy Admiral Hüffmeier, an ardent Nazi who had schemed to undermine his commander's authority. Hüffmeier put loyal naval men into key roles, tried to raise declining troop morale and took a hard line with islanders. People's hopes were pinned on the monthly visit by the *Vega* but spirits were at their lowest ebb. The islands' war could still end very badly.

Liberation

On May 1st 1945 islanders heard that Hitler was dead and knew that the war must be nearly over. People started making flags and wearing badges openly. At 10am on May 8th the Bailiff was told by the Germans that British flags may be flown at 3pm, after Winston Churchill had made a speech on the radio announcing the end of the war in Europe. His speech included the words "…and our dear Channel Islands are also to be freed today."

Operation 'Nestegg' was led by Force 135 under Brigadier Snow, supported by Civil Affairs Unit 20 whose role it was to get normal life restored. In addition to essential supplies it would carry stock for the shops and money for the banks.

HMS *Bulldog* sailed to Guernsey and met with a German trawler off Les Hanois on the 8th. Admiral Hüffmeier sent only a junior officer to discuss terms of an armistice, but Brigadier Snow made clear there would be no negotiation, only unconditional surrender. At 7.14am on May 9th, Hüffmeier's second in command Generalmajor Heine signed the surrender document on board *Bulldog* anchored off St Peter Port. The swastika flags on the German boats were replaced by the White Ensign and a small advance party led by Lt Colonel Stoneman went ashore at the Cambridge Steps to be met by enthusiastic crowds. Later in the afternoon, another 200 troops arrived by landing craft at Havelet Bay. RAF aircraft flew past in salute.

(top & right)
British officers accept the unconditional surrender of the German garrison.

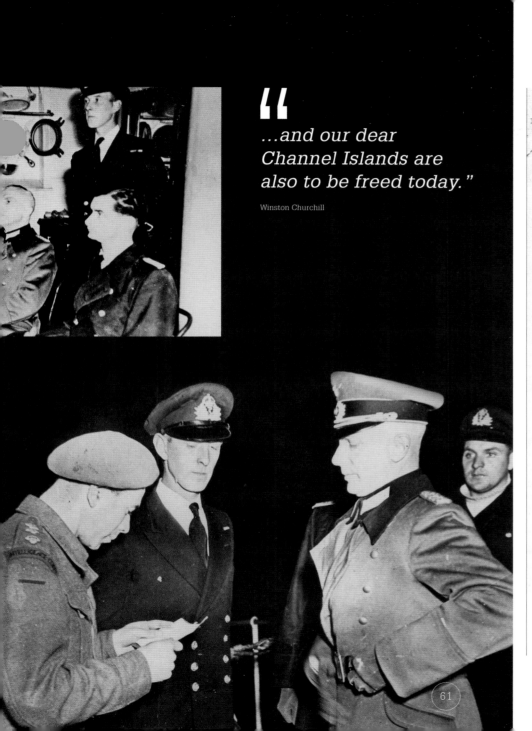

> **"**
> *...and our dear Channel Islands are also to be freed today."*
>
> Winston Churchill

Der Befehlshaber der deutschen Streitkräfte
auf den Kanalinseln.   8.Mai 1945.

An den
        Brigadier und Vertreter des Obersten Alliierten
                    Befehlshabers.

I. Auf Ihren Brief vom 8.Mai 1945 bestätige ich Ihnen meinen
   Funkspruch an Sie wie folgt:
   "An den Brigadier und Vertreter des Obersten Alliierten
   Befehlshabers auf "H 91" über MTI.

        1.) Ich bestätige Ihren Brief vom 8.Mai.
        2.) Mein bevollmächtigter Vertreter, Generalmajor Heine,
            wird um 24.00 Uhr deutscher Sommerzeit Ihnen an der
            gleichen Zusammenkunftstelle begegnen.
        3.) Für sichere Anfahrt stehe ich ein.
                            Befehlshaber der deutschen Truppen auf
                                    den Kanalinseln."
II. Ich hatte der englischen Bevölkerung gestattet, am heutigen
    Nachmittag zu flaggen und Dankgottesdienste abzuhalten und
    musste daher damit rechnen, dass eine gewisse Unruhe unter
    meinen Soldaten entstehen konnte. Dies ist tatsächlich der
    Fall gewesen. Ich war und bin daher nicht in der Lage, selbst
    mich mit Ihnen zu treffen.
III. Zu den einzelnen Punkten der Bestimmungen zur Durchführung
     der Übergabe bemerke ich, dass meine Archive und Akten bereits
     während des Abgeschnittenseins der Kanalinseln laufend und
     planmässig vernichtet worden sind, sodass ich über Akten und
     Archive nicht mehr verfüge.
IV. Ich schlage vor, die Entwaffnung meiner Soldaten erst am
    9.5. bei Helligkeit durchzuführen, da bei der Betriebsstoff-
    lage der Festungen die Unterkünfte ohne Licht sind. Die
    Entwaffnung wird daher bei Nacht zu meines Erachtens uner-
    wünschten Schwierigkeiten führen.
 V. Über Flugzeuge verfüge ich nicht.

                                        Vizeadmiral

Letter signed by Vizeadmiral Hüffmeier regarding terms of the surrender.

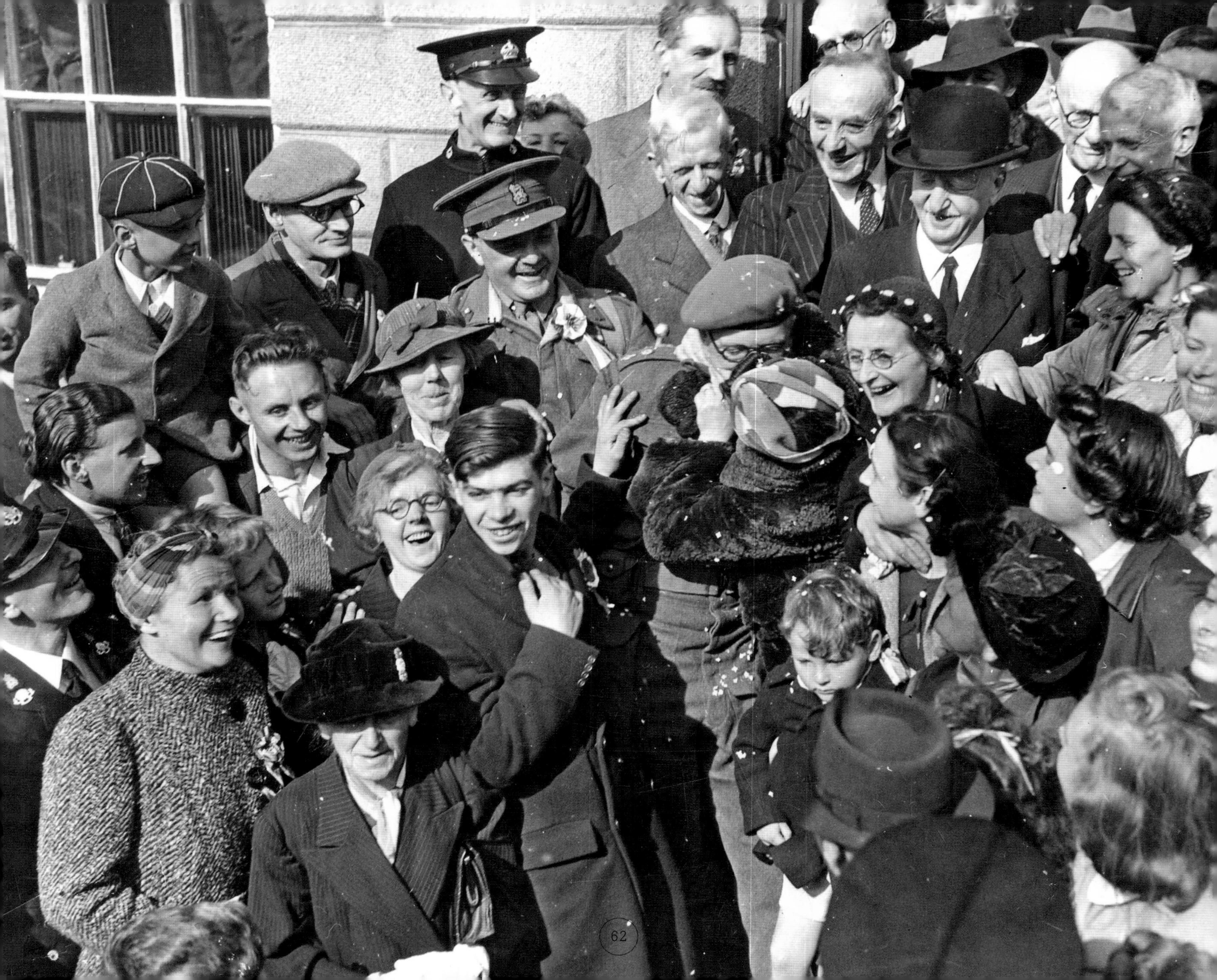

Sark was liberated the following day, but as the British had no troops to spare the Dame was asked to take charge. For a week she had 275 Germans under her command and ordered them to start tidying up the island. The main 'Nestegg' force began landing on the 14th, when Brigadier Snow accepted Hüffmeier's formal surrender. He marched to the Royal Court, then on to Elizabeth College where he read out a Royal Proclamation from the King cheered by crowds. There was no cheering in Alderney where only a sullen garrison of 2,332 men remained awaiting imprisonment when British troops landed on the 16th.

(above & left)
Brigadier Snow reads the Royal Proclamation at Elizabeth College

(far left)
Enthusiastic crowds greet liberating British troops.

Evacuees celebrated in whatever town they found themselves, and the news of liberation reached service personnel scattered across the world, whilst freed deportees, prisoners, and PoWs awaited their return home. The final act of the Liberation took place on June 7th, when King George VI and Queen Elizabeth visited Guernsey and received a Loyal Address from the Bailiff. The islands were free once more.

(above)
Force 135's main contingent arrives.

(right)
Deportees at Biberach taste freedom at last.

(above)
An island boy enjoys a taste of chocolate.

(left)
DUKW motors to the slipway by the Connaught Steps.

(right)
Mrs Elsie Jory celebrates Liberation in St Peter Port.

Carel Toms

Aftermath

Liberation ended the only period that Guernsey had been occupied by foreign troops for six centuries, but the Occupation continued to cast a shadow for years to come. The islands had escaped most of the cruelty and destruction suffered by other countries in Europe, but their beautiful scenery had been left a mess of military installations, abandoned weapons, barbed wire and minefields, with their population scattered.

Evacuees were only allowed to return in batches, as they first needed homes and jobs. Some indeed had married in Britain or found good jobs or homes they liked and stayed there. The schools came back during the summer. Families and friends were reunited after five years' separation, but it was not always a happy reunion. There was tension between those who had remained to keep the island running, and those who had endured bombing or done war work in England. Deportees had a different experience again, returning looking well-fed and suntanned in comparison to the half-starved islanders. Men and women who had served in the armed forces were demobilised progressively, although some were still needed to face emergencies in Greece or Palestine or across what was still the Empire. Those who had been in Nazi prisons and concentration camps

had long periods of recovery in hospitals before returning to the Islands.

Alderney was in a sorry state. Homes had been used as billets for the troops, ransacked and looted. It remained under military supervision, with German prisoners put to work making good the damage and removing the minefields. Once advance parties had made preparations, 110 islanders returned after a stormy crossing on December 15th 1945, now marked as Homecoming Day. By the end of 1946 only a third of the population had returned and the economy stumbled; even by 1947 there were only 800 islanders. Although its cows had largely been evacuated to Guernsey, Alderney had to virtually start building its economy from scratch. Furniture and other possessions that had been salvaged in the war and since locked up was arrayed on the hill called Les Butes where people took what they claimed was theirs. Arguments flared over who owned what and bitterness over 'The Battle of the Butes'

Civilians inspect abandoned German fortifications.

lasted for decades. No war crimes trial was held in Alderney itself, but a small number of the men responsible for acts of brutality there were killed later in the war, died in prison or committed suicide. A pair of OT men were sentenced to lengthy imprisonment by the French, but other perpetrators were simply let go without charge by the Allies.

A small proportion of island residents had behaved badly during the Occupation and there were demands that the 'traitors' and profiteers meet justice. Official investigations into collaboration with the enemy ended with a decision by Whitehall that there were to be no trials, causing resentment and allegations of a cover-up. Informants who had betrayed their neighbours, sometimes resulting in their deaths, went unpunished. However, the leading black marketeers and the few who had done well financially were hit by a 60% tax on all wartime profits under £10,000 and 100% above this. There were no violent reprisals against 'Jerrybags'

Rat-infested German sheds at Lager Ursula, a former OT labour camp in St Sampsons, are burned.

Guernsey Press

as seen in neighbouring France, nor against other 'collaborators'; they were simply shunned, and the most brazen culprits left the island.

Those who had resisted the occupiers were not treated as heroes, indeed their courage was even regarded as foolishly endangering other islanders. It took much campaigning by GUNS reporter Frank Falla for those imprisoned or maltreated by the Germans to receive compensation. Some 50 victims finally received money in 1966, but many more were excluded including the deportees. The dismissed policemen were not forgiven for their defiance of the Germans and the majority of their wartime convictions in the Royal Court were allowed to stand, despite legal appeals. Some still regard this as a travesty of justice and plans are made from time to time to have the convictions quashed and the men's good name restored.

Island government had to be re-organised, the economy was in a poor state and the financial position dire. The British government gave a grant, but this largely went to settle bank debts and overdue salaries. Guernsey's horticulture industry recovered quickly, and most of its cattle herds had survived the war. Tourism also began to flourish. One unseen impact of Occupation was the fatal blow it struck against the island languages. With so many children evacuated or born away from the island, English became their daily language. Adult evacuees and those serving in the forces were speaking English routinely, and many married non-islanders during or straight after the war. Guernésiais entered a steep decline in Guernsey, whilst Aurignais and Sercquiais would become extinct as spoken languages by the end of the century.

Memorial

The Occupation holds an important place in the minds of islanders and frames the modern history of the Bailiwick of Guernsey. However, at the end of the war the overwhelming urge was to move ahead with life and forget the unpleasantness. Only as the Occupation became history, did people become ready for commemorations and memorials.

Liberation Day has been celebrated as a national holiday in Guernsey every year since the war, and since 1970 has taken place on May 9th. It has grown in popularity to become a festival with parades, floats, food, music and nostalgic events following a formal church service of remembrance. Although aimed squarely at locals, it has become a tourist draw early in the season. Sark celebrates on May 10th, but Alderney has no 'Liberation Day' so instead 'Homecoming Day' is a more sedate affair marked in the depth of winter on December 15th. The dark legacy of Nazi crimes in Alderney still throws a shadow on that island's approach to the Occupation.

Particularly poignant is Charybdis Day, where the Royal Navy sends a ship and a contingent of sailors for a service at the Foulon Cemetery around the anniversary on October 23rd. The deportees and the evacuees also hold their own commemorations. Links have been forged with British cities that accepted

refugees and a strong friendship has grown up between Guernsey and Biberach, with annual exchange visits carrying the theme of reconciliation.

Names of the 223 servicemen from Guernsey, 25 from Alderney and one from Sark who died in the war were added to the islands' war memorials along with the greater number lost in the First World War.

Further memorials began to spring up, principally at St Peter Port harbour. A memorial to the 34 people killed in the harbour bombing was erected in 1949 and a stone to commemorate the landing of the first British troops was installed at Connaught Steps on the 40th anniversary of Liberation in 1985. The Liberation Monument designed by Eric Snell was erected to mark the 50th anniversary in 1995, followed by a stone placed close by and unveiled by Queen Elizabeth II in 2005 and another by

(top left)
Blue Plaque commemorating the GUNS team.

(above)
Allied Air Crew Memorial at Guernsey Airport.

(right)
The Shell Shrine created in a German bunker at Fort Hommet, made entirely from seashells.

(left)
Island War Memorial.

VisitGuernsey

(above)
The Liberation Memorial erected in 1995, beside the Weighbridge restored after damage in the bombing of 1940.

the Countess of Wessex in 2015. The area has been re-named 'Piace de la Liberation' and is a focus for remembrance. Controversially a memorial to the Foreign Workers who died during the Occupation erected in 1999 had to be re-carved with revised wording in 2001. A bronze plaque to the three murdered Jewish women was placed in 2001 and has become the site for a service on Holocaust Memorial Day. A plaque was erected to the deportees in 2010, naming those who did not return, and one for the evacuees also in 2010. The last memorial of the group at the harbour installed in 2015 was to the islanders who died for their acts of protest, defiance and resistance, although only seven are named with space for an eighth to be added when the time is right. A stone dedicated to French workers installed in Alderney in 1951 was replaced in 1967 by the Hammond Memorial, remembering the hundreds of slave workers who suffered and died on the island.

Guernsey initiated a blue plaque scheme to recognise people who had made significant contributions to island life, and amongst those recognised so far have been resister Major Marie Ozanne, Herbert Le Patourel VC and the team behind GUNS. An inspiring new Allied Aircrew memorial was created in 2015 outside Guernsey Airport to remember the 153 airmen who lost their lives in the skies above the islands, and a piece of public art was commissioned from sculptor Mark Cook to celebrate the 75th anniversary of Liberation in 2020.

Many households kept personal photographs, letters, diaries and a few souvenirs left behind by Germans they had grown to know. Few people were interested in the relics of the war in the immediate aftermath and much German material was taken away for scrap. However, a small number of enterprising individuals started collecting weapons, helmets, equipment and the ephemera of Occupation such as identity cards and posters. As interest in the war years revived, museums or heritage sites started to open up, most notably the German Underground Hospital in 1954 and the German Occupation Museum founded by Richard Heaume MBE in 1966. The Occupation now forms an important feature of the tourist industry.

photos: VisitGuernsey

(above)
The Countess of Wessex unveils a memorial marking 70 years of freedom in 2015.

(right)
Detail of Mark Cook's original clay sculpture for his 75th anniversary of Liberation public artwork.

(far right)
Liberation Day celebrations in St Peter Port always attract large crowds.

Mark Cook

A challenge for heritage professionals is how to preserve the dozens of German fortifications that now form part of Guernsey and Alderney's unique historic landscape, and indeed decide which cannot be saved from decay. A further challenge is to avoid the sites becoming shrines to the Nazis, and to honestly tell the story of the occupiers and the occupied, the oppressors and the oppressed. Stories of courage, unexpected friendships and sheer perseverance should not be forgotten.

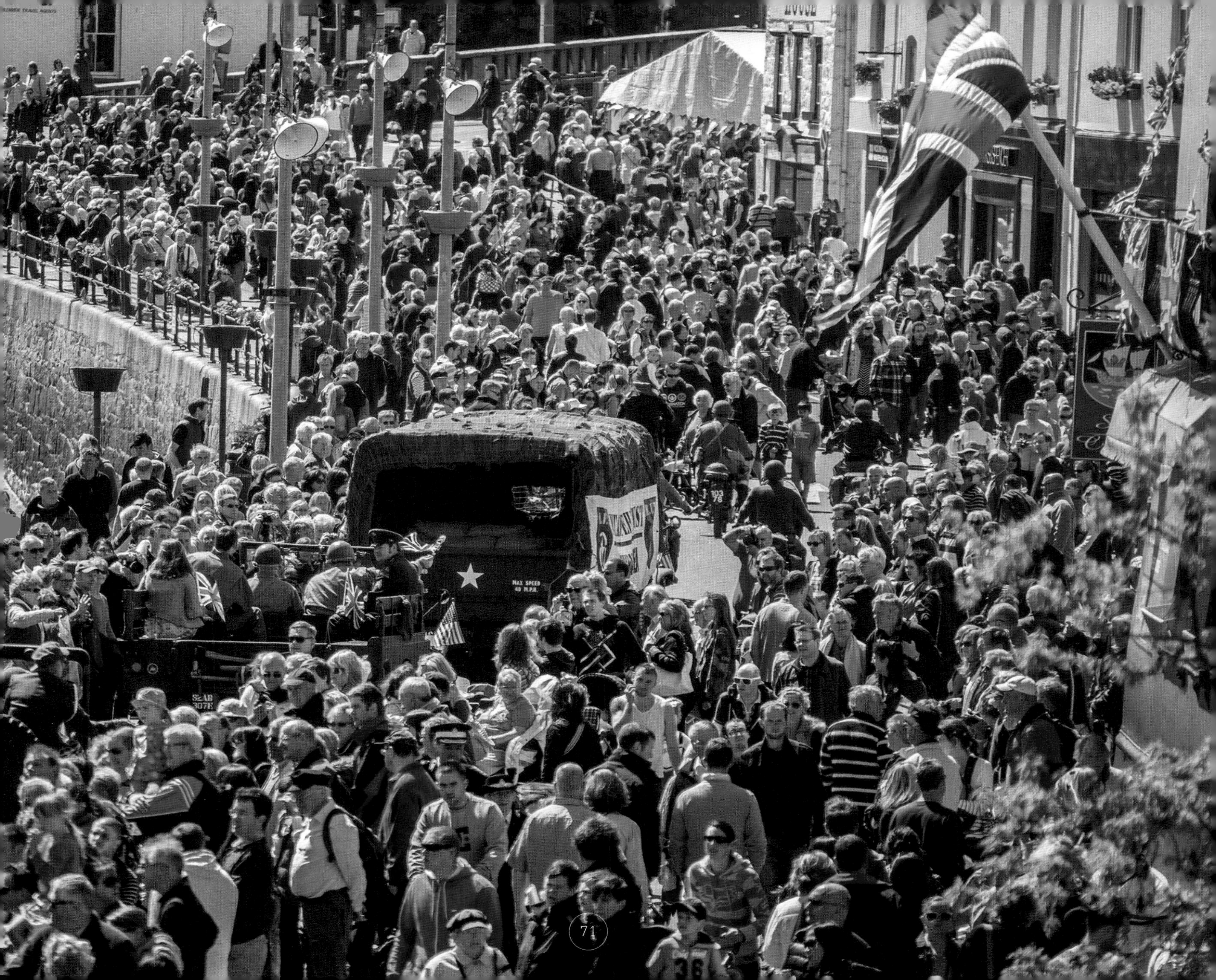
MAX SPEED
40 M.P.H.

Fact and Fiction

The Second World War continues to be a source of fascination, and the occupation of the Channel Islands has spawned literally hundreds of factual books, magazines articles, novels, television documentaries and feature films. The British are fond of nostalgia and from wanting to forget the war years, islanders have swung around to preserving the memory of that time.

Specialist books abound, particularly covering fortifications and weapons, and histories of the police and medical services. Following from Charles Cruickshank's Official History *The German Occupation of the Channel Islands,* a fair number of amateur historians have written their own histories of the occupation, often via small presses or self-published so these books can be hard to find outside the islands. Academic works appearing 70 years after the event started addressing more difficult aspects of the war such as resistance and treatment of the Jews but some subjects are still almost out of bounds, in particular collaboration. Journalist Madeleine Bunting's *The Model Occupation* was criticised

in detail for its unbalanced portrayal and negative light it cast on islanders. Unfortunately, there are also occasional sensational pieces about Nazi activities in the islands, both in print and on satellite TV channels.

Fictional stories of the war years heavily mine true events for inspiration, including the most sinister section of Guernsey's most-loved novel, *The Book of Ebenezer Le Page*. Perhaps the grittiest occupation novel is the mystery-thriller *Island Madness* by Tim Binding. It includes the plotline of a local woman involved with a German soldier, which becomes an over-used idea in fiction including in the incredibly popular *The Guernsey Literary and Potato Peel Pie Society*. That book also uses the device of secrets emerging after the war as seen in Mary Horlock's *The Book of Lies* and Michael Crouch's trilogy *My Enemy is My Friend*. Wartime Alderney is the fictional base of operations in Jack Higgins' *The Eagle Has Landed* and he set *Night of the Fox* in Jersey. Dr Who even intervenes to thwart Nazi plans in Guernsey in Lance Parkin's *Just War*.

Rescuing a cow from wartime Sark is the plot of the gentle 1951 film *Appointment With Venus*. The island was called 'Amorel' in the film and was inspired by the saving of the Alderney herd. *Triple Cross* (1966) is based on the 'true story' of Eddie Chapman recruited from a Jersey prison to become a German agent. The 1973 Peter Sellers film *The Blockhouse* was filmed

Props from the STUDIOCANAL movie *The Guernsey Literary and Potato Peel Pie Society* on display at Guernsey Museum.

entirely in Guernsey, although set in France around D-Day. *Enemy at the Door* was an ITV series centred on a Guernsey doctor and his delicate relations with the Occupiers that ran for 26 episodes from 1978 to 1980. Largely set-bound, its exterior scenes were shot in Jersey. *Islands at War* was an expensive 2004 ITV series that attempted to merge stories from all the islands and set them on fictional 'St George'. Filmed on the Isle of Man it was criticised for straining historical accuracy too far and was cancelled after just 6 episodes. The Alderney segments of The *Eagle Has Landed* (1976) were not filmed there, and to much local consternation none of the 2017 film of *The Guernsey Literary and Potato Peel Pie Society* was filmed in the islands. Events from the War also crop up as plot drivers in the long-running 1980s TV detective series *Bergerac*. Although Somerset doubles for Jersey perhaps the most realistic portrayal of the Occupation is given in *Another Mother's Son*, closely based on the true story of a family who hid an escaped slave worker.

The unique circumstance of German troops occupying British soil sustains interest in the Occupation into the 21st century. After the war, a steady stream of memoirs and diaries started to be published by people who lived through Occupation, evacuation or deportation. Some authors were children at the time who did not fully understand what was happening around them or could barely remember when the islands were free. Stories of tricks played by islanders to seize food, cheek the Germans or hide secret radios can come over as comic. Making light of desperate times can make the Occupation sound like a bit of an adventure, armed with hindsight over how the war ended, but memoirs such as Frank Falla's *The Silent War* show what a dark time it was.

Selected Bibliography

Richard Allisette Islanders in Kitbags
William M Bell I Beg to Report
Molly Bihet A Child's War
Molly Bihet A Time for Memories
Madeleine Bunting The Model Occupation
Gilly Cárr, Paul Sanders and Louise Wilmott Protest, Defiance and Resistance in the Channel Islands
Charles Cruickshank The German Occupation of the Channel Islands
Trevor Davenport Festung Alderney
Ralph Durand Guernsey under German Rule
Frank Falla The Silent War
Roger E Harris Islanders Deported
June Money Aspects of War
M. J. Packe and M Dreyfuss The Alderney Story 1939/45
T.X.H Pantcheff Alderney Fortress Island
Winston Ramsey The War in the Channel Islands Then and Now
Brian Ahier Read No Cause For Panic

Festung Guernsey is a massive and finely illustrated work compiled by the Germans, possibly with the intention of presenting Hitler with a detailed compendium of his only British conquest. It is available as a facsimile reproduction with English translation.

Museum exhibition publications On British Soil, Nazi Persecution in the Channel Islands and Occupied Behind Barbed Wire, were written by Gilly Carr, who also compiled the online Frank Falla Archive.

The Channel Islands Occupation Review published annually by the Channel Islands Occupation Society contains a wealth of original information, particularly on fortifications and the reminiscences of islanders and German soldiers.

A number of websites may also be found online.

Acknowledgements

Completion of this book has been made possible with the assistance of the Alderney Society, Lisa Burton, Visit Alderney, Visit Guernsey and the author is grateful for comments received on the draft text from Paul Bourgaize, Gilly Carr, Trevor Davenport

Guernsey Museum Production team

Designed by Paul le Tissier
Image Editor Lisa Burton

About the Author

Dr Jason Monaghan is an archaeologist, historian and novelist. He was Director of Museums for Guernsey then Head of Heritage Services from 2006 to 2019.

first edition
May 2020